Git Best Practices Guide

Master the best practices of Git with the help of
real-time scenarios to maximize team efficiency
and workflow

Eric Pidoux

BIRMINGHAM - MUMBAI

Git Best Practices Guide

First published: November 2014

Production reference: 1141114

Published by Packt Publishing Ltd.
Livery Place
35 Livery Street
Birmingham B3 2PB, UK.

ISBN 978-1-78355-373-0

www.packtpub.com

Credits

Author
Eric Pidoux

Reviewers
Paulo Alcantara
Edward E Griebel Jr
Scott M. Spear

Commissioning Editor
Dipika Gaonkar

Acquisition Editor
Llewellyn Rozario

Content Development Editor
Melita Lobo

Technical Editors
Pratik More
Humera Shaikh

Copy Editor
Sayanee Mukherjee

Project Coordinator
Kinjal Bari

Proofreaders
Paul Hindle
Samantha Lyon

Indexer
Hemangini Bari

Graphics
Ronak Dhruv
Valentina D'silva
Disha Haria
Abhinash Sahu

Production Coordinator
Melwyn D'sa

Cover Work
Melwyn D'sa

About the Author

Eric Pidoux has a Master's degree in Computer Science from Miage Aix-Marseille and is currently working as a lead web developer at createur.ch, Lausanne, Switzerland. He started learning PHP 10 years ago and is now a Symfony2 ninja who likes coding as well as drinking beer.

He has worked as a technical reviewer on *GitLab Repository Management* and *Extending Symfony2 Web Application Framework*, both by Packt Publishing.

> I would like to dedicate this book to my father and thank all my friends and, of course, my awesome family.

About the Reviewers

Paulo Alcantara is a software engineer at C.E.S.A.R, a company based in Recife, Brazil. He works on UEFI firmware development, where he has an equivalent experience of over 4 years. His previous employers include Intel Corporation, Nokia Institute of Technology, and ProFUSION embedded systems. He graduated from high school and is a free software hacker who is interested in filesystems, storages, bootloaders, operating systems, and BIOS/UEFI firmware. He has experience working with C, C++, x86 assembly language, Python, Lisp, Perl, and Bash. He is the author of NTFS and XFS filesystem drivers of the SYSLINUX bootloader. He is also the excore developer of the PySide project and contributed to BlueZ (Linux Bluetooth stack) and Enlightenment Foundation Libraries (EFL). Currently, in his free time, he works on a BSD-licensed UEFI driver for the UDF/ECMA-167 filesystem.

I would like to thank my team and project manager at C.E.S.A.R (Victor Gouveia, Mauro Faccenda, Thiago Carneiro, Carlos Leal, and Tarciana Mello) and my parents, especially my mother (Morgana Oliveira) who made me enough coffee to get the review on this book done.

Edward E Griebel Jr has been developing enterprise software for over 20 years in C, C++, and Java. He has a Bachelor of Science degree in Computer Engineering. He is currently a middleware architect at a leading payroll and financial services provider in the US, focusing on systems integration and UI and server development.

Scott M. Spear owns and operates Webmasters by Design LLC, a web design and development business. He has a Bachelor of Science degree in Computer Management Information Systems and a Master of Business Administration degree, with over a decade of web design, development, and hosting experience. He has experience in a variety of areas, including web design, development, and hosting, and he also specializes in dynamic website design and development, using technologies such as PHP, MySQL, CSS, Ajax, jQuery, and Zend Framework. Additionally, Scott is experienced in Photoshop, Dreamweaver, WordPress, and Joomla!.

www.PacktPub.com

Support files, eBooks, discount offers, and more

You might want to visit www.PacktPub.com for support files and downloads related to your book.

Did you know that Packt offers eBook versions of every book published, with PDF and ePub files available? You can upgrade to the eBook version at www.PacktPub.com and as a print book customer, you are entitled to a discount on the eBook copy. Get in touch with us at service@packtpub.com for more details.

At www.PacktPub.com, you can also read a collection of free technical articles, sign up for a range of free newsletters and receive exclusive discounts and offers on Packt books and eBooks.

http://PacktLib.PacktPub.com

Do you need instant solutions to your IT questions? PacktLib is Packt's online digital book library. Here, you can access, read and search across Packt's entire library of books.

Why subscribe?

- Fully searchable across every book published by Packt
- Copy and paste, print and bookmark content
- On demand and accessible via web browser

Free access for Packt account holders

If you have an account with Packt at www.PacktPub.com, you can use this to access PacktLib today and view nine entirely free books. Simply use your login credentials for immediate access.

Table of Contents

Preface

Git is a decentralized versioning system that was created by Linus Torvalds (also the creator of Linux Kernel) under the GNU license. It was developed to be simple and efficient. Its aim is to manage the content evolution of a file tree.

This book is an easy-to-follow guide to understand the basic to the deepest levels of Git's abilities. As a Git user (beginner or experienced), you will face some basic questions, such as: how do you find the code you changed just a few weeks ago? Is it possible to work with other team members using Git? In case of conflict, how can I resolve it?

Git Best Practices Guide will help you to answer these questions by increasing your skills on Git (learning a practical way to use Git commands with examples).

If you are an SVN user, we will also see how it is possible to easily migrate an SVN repository to Git with a step-by-step guide.

Starting with the basics of Git, this book will lead you to the advanced features, making you more self confident when there are merge conflicts or issues while finding content.

The last part of this book will teach you how to improve your workflow using Git. More and more companies or team members use Agile as a workflow process, leaving behind old-fashioned processes such as waterfall, cascade, iterative enhancement, and so on. As a versioning system, Git has to be a part of this process. In this book, we will see how to take your workflow to another level by creating an efficient branching system, using Continuous Integration, and discovering repository managers.

What this book covers

Chapter 1, *Starting a Git Repository*, covers the basics of Git, describing how to create a repository and start committing files.

Chapter 2, *Working in a Team Using Git*, explains the best practices to work with other developers as a team by pointing out the useful commands.

Chapter 3, *Finding and Resolving Conflicts*, covers all tips and commands that are useful to fix mistakes, resolve conflicts, search inside the commit history, and so on.

Chapter 4, *Going Deeper into Git*, explains the hard commands or not-so-commonly-used commands such as applying patch, using submodules, and migrating from SVN.

Chapter 5, *Using Git for Continuous Integration*, explains how to improve the team workflow by using Continuous Integration.

What you need for this book

To run commands provided in this book, you need the Git software.

Who this book is for

If you are a Git user (beginner or experienced), you want to learn all Git features without heavy theory, or you need to have a practical book to use Git, then this book is for you.

Conventions

In this book, you will find a number of styles of text that distinguish between different kinds of information. Here are some examples of these styles, and an explanation of their meaning.

Code words in text, database table names, folder names, filenames, file extensions, pathnames, dummy URLs, user input, and Twitter handles are shown as follows: "If the repository is `public`, it will create a folder and everything inside the folder."

Any command-line input or output is written as follows:

```
Erik@server:~/git/myRepoName$ git log
commit df9448ff53864d8cfc6f78fd8831fd363d63a28b
Author: Erik <erik@mymail.com>
Date:    Thu July 10 06:44:47 2014 +0000
```

New terms and important words are shown in bold. Words that you see on the screen, in menus or dialog boxes for example, appear in the text like this: "Click on **Begin Import**."

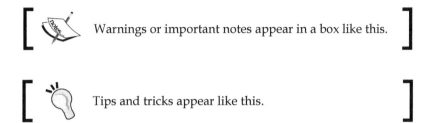

Warnings or important notes appear in a box like this.

Tips and tricks appear like this.

Reader feedback

Feedback from our readers is always welcome. Let us know what you think about this book—what you liked or may have disliked. Reader feedback is important for us to develop titles that you really get the most out of.

To send us general feedback, simply send an e-mail to feedback@packtpub.com, and mention the book title via the subject of your message.

If there is a topic that you have expertise in and you are interested in either writing or contributing to a book, see our author guide on www.packtpub.com/authors.

Customer support

Now that you are the proud owner of a Packt book, we have a number of things to help you to get the most from your purchase.

Errata

Although we have taken every care to ensure the accuracy of our content, mistakes do happen. If you find a mistake in one of our books—maybe a mistake in the text or the code—we would be grateful if you would report this to us. By doing so, you can save other readers from frustration and help us improve subsequent versions of this book. If you find any errata, please report them by visiting http://www.packtpub.com/submit-errata, selecting your book, clicking on the **errata submission form** link, and entering the details of your errata. Once your errata are verified, your submission will be accepted and the errata will be uploaded on our website, or added to any list of existing errata, under the Errata section of that title. Any existing errata can be viewed by selecting your title from http://www.packtpub.com/support.

Piracy

Piracy of copyright material on the Internet is an ongoing problem across all media. At Packt, we take the protection of our copyright and licenses very seriously. If you come across any illegal copies of our works, in any form, on the Internet, please provide us with the location address or website name immediately so that we can pursue a remedy.

Please contact us at copyright@packtpub.com with a link to the suspected pirated material.

We appreciate your help in protecting our authors, and our ability to bring you valuable content.

Questions

You can contact us at questions@packtpub.com if you are having a problem with any aspect of the book, and we will do our best to address it.

1
Starting a Git Repository

This chapter covers the basics needed to understand the topics discussed in this book, and of course, to improve your skills in Git. Commands in this chapter are used every day by all Git users. Some of them will not be explained in detail; they will be explained in another chapter.

In this chapter, you will learn about:

- Initializing a repository
- Cloning an existing repository
- Adding and committing files
- Pushing commits on remote repositories

Configuring Git

Before you start working on Git, you have to configure your name and e-mail by using the following commands:

```
Erik@local:~$git config --global user.name "Erik"
Erik@local:~$git config --global user.email erik@domain.com
```

Initializing a new repository

If you want to create a repository in an existing project, just type the following command line:

```
Erik@local:~$ cd myProject
Erik@local:~/myProject$ git init .
```

Otherwise, you have to create an empty directory and type `git init` inside it, as shown:

```
Erik@local:~$ mkdir myProject
Erik@local:~$ cd myProject
Erik@local:~/myProject$ git init
```

This will create a folder named `.git` inside the current directory that contains the following files used by Git:

- `Config`: This is used with the configuration for the local Git repository
- `HEAD`: This lists a file that is the current head branch
- `Refs directory`: This contains references to a commit for a branch

Cloning an existent repository

With Git, it is possible to clone an existent repository to work on it.

There are several possibilities to clone a repository, but the `http`, `git`, and `ssh` protocols are used the most.

If the repository is `public`, it will create a folder and everything inside the folder. However, if the repository is `private` or `protected`, you have to enter an access information or provide a private `ssh` key. For example, if you want to clone a `Symfony2` repository, type this line to clone it using `myProjectName` as the folder name:

```
Erik@local:~/myProject$ git clone https://github.com/symfony/symfony.
gitmyProjectName
Initialized empty Git repository in /var/www/myProjectName/.git/
remote: Counting objects: 7820, done.
remote: Compressing objects: 100% (2490/2490), done.
remote: Total 7820 (delta 4610), reused 7711 (delta 4528)
Receiving objects: 100% (7820/7820), 1.40 MiB | 479 KiB/s, done.
Resolving deltas: 100% (4610/4610), done.
Checking out files: 100% (565/565), done.
```

 Note that the name after the `clone` command is optional. If there is no parameter after the repository location, the repository name will be used.

You probably read the line about compressing objects. In fact, before sending any content, Git compresses objects to speed the transmission.

We will see more uses of the `clone` command in the next chapter.

Working with the repository

We have to take a few minutes to look at the life cycle of a file inside Git.

A file will go through the following states, and the Git command line will take the file from one state to another. We will explain each state and its command line.

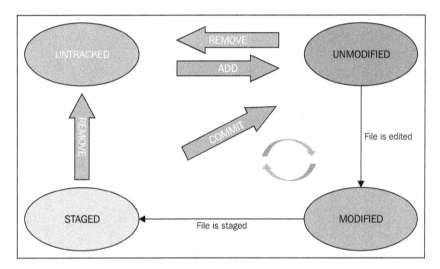

The important part of this schema is the triangle between the three states **UNMODIFIED**, **MODIFIED**, and **STAGED**. This triangle is an infinite loop. Indeed, every time you change a file, its state is set to modified, and then staged; when you commit the file, it returns to the unmodified state, and so on.

UNTRACKED is the first state where the file is created, but this isn't tracked by Git.

To change the state of a file, you have to add it.

Adding a file

When you start an empty repository and add a file, it will be in the untracked state, which means that it isn't in the Git repository.

To track a file, you have to execute this command line:

```
Erik@local:~/myProject$ touch MyFileName.txt
Erik@local:~/myProject$ echo "test" > MyFileName.txt
Erik@local:~/myProject$ git add MyFileName.txt
```

So, your file is now tracked by Git.

If you want to add all files because you already have something inside the directory while you create the repository, add a period (.) just after git add to specify to take all files inside the current directory:

```
Erik@local:~/myProject$ echo "hello" > MyFile2.txt
Erik@local:~/myProject$ echo "hello" > MyFile3.txt
Erik@local:~/myProject$ git add .
```

The file is currently staged and ready to be committed inside the repository.

Committing a file

As soon as your file is tracked, all changes will be notified by Git, and you have to commit the change on the repository.

 Remember to commit your change as soon as possible (not for every line, but it's a marker to validate what you have done).

The commit command is local to your own repository, nobody except you can see it.

The commit command line offers various options. For example, you can commit a file, as shown in the following example:

```
Erik@local:~/myProject$ git commit -m 'This message explains the changes'
MyFileName.txt
```

To commit everything, use the following command:

```
Erik@local:~/myProject$ git commit -m 'My commit message'
```

You will create a new commit object in the Git repository. This commit is referenced by an SHA-1 checksum and includes various data (content files, content directories, the commit history, the committer, and so on). You can show this information by executing the following command line:

```
Erik@local:~/myProject$ git log
```

It will display something similar to the following:

```
Commit f658e5f22afe12ce75cde1h671b58d6703ab83f5
Author: Eric Pidoux <contact@eric-pidoux.com>
Date: Mon Jun 2 22:54:04 2014 +0100
My commit message
```

The file is in the unmodified state because you just committed the change; you can push the files in the remote repository.

Pushing a file

Once committed, you can push the files in the remote repository. It can be on a bare repository, using init with the git init --bare command, so just type the following command:

```
Erik@local:~/myProject$ git push /home/erik/remote-repository.git
```

If you create a remote repository on another server, you have to configure your local Git repository.

If you use Git 2.0 or later, the previous command will print out something like this on the screen:

```
Warning: push.default is unset; its implicit value is changing in
Git 2.0 from 'matching' to 'simple'. To squelch this message
and maintain the current behavior after the default changes, use:
gitconfig --global push.default matching
To squelch this message and adopt the new behavior now, use:
gitconfig --global push.default simple
```

The 'matching' value from the push.default configuration variable denotes that git push will push all your local branches to the branches with the same name on the remote. This makes it easy to accidentally push a branch you didn't intend to.

The 'simple' value from the push.default configuration variable denotes that git push will push only the current branch to the branch that git pull will pull from; it also checks that their names match. This is a more intuitive behavior, which is why the default should be changed to this configuration value.

Firstly, check if a remote repository is defined:

```
Erik@local:~/myProject$ git remote
```

If it's not, define the remote repository named origin:

```
Erik@local:~/myProject$ git remote add origin http://github.com/
myRepoAddress.git
```

Now, push the changes using the following command:

```
Erik@local:~/myProject$ git push -u origin master
```

After this, you will have a resume of what was pushed.

In fact, the remote repository will check the current Head (the reference to the commit) and compare it with its own. If there are differences between them, it will fail.

Removing a file

If you don't want a file anymore, there are two ways to remove it:

- Delete the file manually and commit the changes. This will delete the file locally and on the repository. Use the following command line

  ```
  Erik@local:~/myProject$ git commit -m 'delete this file'
  ```

- Delete the file only through Git:

  ```
  Erik@local:~/myProject$ git rm --cached MyFileName.txt
  ```

Checking the status

There is a way to display the working tree status, that is, the files that have changed and those that need to be pushed, and of course, there is a way to display the conflicts:

```
Erik@local:~/myProject$ git status
```

If everything is correct and up to date, you will get this result:

```
Erik@local:~/myProject$ git status
# On branch master
nothing to commit, working directory clean
```

If you add a file, Git will warn you to track it by using the `git add` command:

```
Erik@local:~/myProject$ touch text5.txt
Erik@local:~/myProject$ git status
# On branch master
# Untracked files:
#   (use "git add <file>..." to include in what will be committed)
#
#     text5.txt
nothing added to commit but untracked files present (use "git add" to
track)
```

If you edit `MyFile2.txt` and type `git status` again, then you will have new lines:

```
Erik@local:~/myProject$ echo "I am changing this file" > MyFile2.txt
Erik@local:~/myProject$ git status
# On branch master
# Changes to be committed:
#   (use "gitreset HEAD<file>..." to unstage)
#
#     new file: text5.txt
#
# Changes not staged for commit:
#   (use "git add <file>…" to update what will be committed)
#
# modified: MyFile2.txt
#
```

On these lines, separate paragraphs display all files in each state. The `MyFile2.txt` file is not tracked by Git and `text5.txt` is ready to be committed.

If you add `text5.txt` using the `git add` command, you will notice the following changes:

```
Erik@local:~/myProject$ git add MyFile2.txt
Erik@local:~/myProject$ git status
# On branch master
# Changes to be committed:
#   (use "git reset HEAD <file>..." to unstage)
#
#     new file:    text5.txt
#     modified:    MyFile2.txt
#
```

Ignoring files

Git can easily ignore some files or folders from your working tree. For example, consider a website on which you are working, and there is an `upload` folder that you might not push on the repository to avoid having test images in your repository.

To do so, create a `.gitignore` file inside the root of your working tree:

```
Erik@local:~/myProject$ touch .gitignore
```

Then, add this line in the file; it will untrack the `upload` folder and its contents:

```
upload
```

Files or folders you define in this file will not be tracked by Git anymore.

You can add some easy regex, such as the following:

- If you want to ignore all PHP files, use the following regex:

  ```
  *.php
  ```

- If you want to ignore all files having p or l at the end of its name, use the following regex:

  ```
  *.[pl]
  ```

- If you want to ignore all temporary files (finishing by ~), use the following regex:

  ```
  *~
  ```

If the file is already pushed on the repository, the file is tracked by Git. To remove it, you will have to use the `git rm command` line by typing this:

```
Erik@local:~/myProject$ git rm --cached MyFileName.txt
```

Summary

In this chapter, we saw the basics of Git: how to create a Git repository, how to put content in it, and how to push data to a remote repository.

In the next chapter, we will see how to use Git with a team and manage all interactions with a remote repository.

Working in a Team Using Git

2

This chapter introduces the aim of Git: team work.

A lot of programmers use Git every day; however often, they are not working alone but as part of a team. Git is a powerful versioning tool to work together, without erasing someone else's content. In the examples of this chapter, we will use the following conditions:

- Three programmers working together on a simple website project
- They install Git, but nothing is created
- They own a dedicated server with Git, SSH, and GitLab installed on it

Creating a server repository

In the first chapter, we saw how to create a simple local Git repository, but now, it's time to create a server repository that will store and manage the code. Of course, for our example, it will be created by GitLab, but not everyone wants GitLab or GitHub.

 A server repository, also called "bare repository", is a Git repository without a working copy.

Git can use four protocols to transport data:

- Local
- Secure Shell (SSH)
- Git
- HTTP

We will see how and when to use these protocols. We will also distinguish between the pros and cons of each protocol.

For all protocols, we have to create the bare repository by executing these lines on the server's command lines.

```
Erik@server:~$ mkdir webproject
#Create the folder
Erik@server:~$ cd webproject
#go inside it
Erik@server:~/webproject$ git init --bare
Initialized empty Git repository in /home/erik/webproject
```

With these commands, we create a directory web project and initialize an empty Git bare repository.

Local

The local protocol is the basic protocol; the remote repository is a local directory. This protocol is used if all members have access to the remote repository (through NFS, for example).

Now, every programmer has to clone it in local:

```
Erik@local:~$ git clone /opt/git/webproject.git
```

For example, we assume that Jim, one of the programmers, has already written some code lines. Jim has to initialize a local Git repository inside the directory and set a remote location for the bare repository:

```
Jim@local:~/webproject$ git init
Jim@local:~/webproject$ git remote add origin /opt/git/webproject.git
```

The following are the pros and cons of the local protocol:

Pros	Cons
Easy to share with other members	Hard to set up a shared network
Fast access on the repository	Fast only if the file access is fast

SSH

Secure Shell (SSH) is the most used protocol, especially if, as in our example, the remote repository is on a distant server.

Now, every programmer has to first clone it in local:

```
Erik@local:~$ git clone ssh://username@server/webproject.git
```

Using the SSH protocol, programmers have to install their SSH keys on the remote repository in order to push to and pull from it. Otherwise, they have to specify the password on each `remote` command.

For our Jim's case:

```
Jim@local:~/webproject$ git init
Jim@local:~/webproject$ git remote add origin ssh://username@server/
webproject.git
```

The following are the pros and cons of the SSH protocol:

Pros	Cons
Easy to share using a remote server	No anonymous access
SSH compresses data while transport, which makes it fast	

Git

The Git transport is similar to SSH, but without any security. You can't push data on it by default, but you can activate this feature. This isn't a good idea at all! Anyone who finds the repository address can push data. Like in all cases, the programmer has to clone it in local, as follows:

```
Erik@local:~$ git clone git://username@server/webproject.git
```

For our Jim's case:

```
Jim@local:~/webproject$ git init
Jim@local:~/webproject$ git remote add origin git://username@server/
webproject.git
```

The following are the pros and cons of the Git transport:

Pros	Cons
Faster than the others	No security (the Git transport is the same as SSH, without the security layer)

HTTPS

The HTTPS protocol is the easiest to set up. Anyone who has access to the web server can clone it.

The programmers start to clone it in local:

```
Erik@local:~$ git clone https://server/webproject.git
```

And, of course, in our Jim's case:

```
Jim@local:~/webproject$ git init .
Jim@local:~/webproject$ git remote add origin http://server/webproject.git
```

Pros	Cons
Easy to set up	Very slow data transport

Pushing data on remote repositories – Jim's case

So, Jim initializes a new Git repository in the directory, where he starts coding, and he adds the remote repository with the SSH protocol. He has to commit and push what he coded earlier. This is how he did it:

```
Jim@local:~/webproject$ git add .
Jim@local:~/webproject$ git commit -m 'add my code'
[master (commit racine) 83fcc8a] add my code
2 files changed, 0 insertions(+), 0 deletions(-)
create mode 100644 index.html
create mode 100644 readme.txt
Jim@local:~/webproject$ git push -u origin master
Counting objects: 3, done.
Compressing objects: 100% (2/2), done.
Writing objects: 100% (3/3), 225 bytes | 0 byte/s, done.
Total 3 (delta 0), reused 0 (delta 0)
```

Now, the remote repository contains two files (index.html and readme.txt).

Pulling data from the repository

The other programmers have to pull data to get the new files.

 Every time you start working on a project, you have to pull data from the remote repository to maintain and ensure that the code is up to date.

The following command is used to pull data:

```
Erik@local:~/webproject$ git pull origin master
```

This command will check and compare your local commit hash to the remote hash. If the remote is the latest, it will try to merge data with the local master branch. This command is the equivalent of executing git fetch (get remote data) and git merge (merge to your branch).

The name of one of our remote repository is origin, and master is the current local branch.

Creating a patch

Let's explain what a patch is with an example. An external programmer was called by Jim to make small fixes in a part of the project, but Jim didn't want to give him access to the repository, thus preventing him from pushing data. So, he decides to make a patch and sends it by e-mail to Jim:

```
External@local:~/webproject$ git format-patch origin patch-webproject.
patch
```

This command will create .patch files per commit and the external programmer will send the e-mail with it. So, he decides to make a patch and send it by e-mail to Jim.

Jim can import the patch by executing this:

```
Jim@local:~/webproject$ git apply /tmp/patch-webproject.patch
```

This command will apply the patch, but it doesn't create commits.

So, to generate a series of commits, use the git am command:

```
Jim@local:~/webproject$ git am /tmp/patch-webproject.patch
```

Working with branches

Git allows you to create branches, that is, named pointers to commits. You can work on different branches independently from each other. The default branch is most often called master.

A branch pointer in Git is 41 bytes large: 40 bytes of characters and an additional new line character. So, it explains why Git is very fast and cheap in terms of resource consumption.

If you decide to work on a branch, you have to checkout the branch. This means that Git restructures the working tree with the content of the commit to which the branch points and moves the HEAD pointer to the new branch.

The first command to know is:

```
Jim@local:~/webproject$ git branch
```

This command will display all available local branches for the repository. Inside the given list, the current working branch has the prefix *.

If you want to see all branches, including the remote branches, you will have to execute the following command:

```
Jim@local:~/webproject$ git branch -a
```

Creating a branch

You can create a branch with the git branch command. This command allows you to create a new branch using a commit. So, Git will create the branch and populate it with the files from the given commit. If you don't provide a commit, it will use the last (or HEAD) commit:

```
Jim@local:~/webproject$ git branch test
```

Checking out a branch

To start using a branch, you have to check it out. If you do so, Git will ignore files from other branches and prepare to listen to changes on specific files only:

```
Jim@local:~/webproject$ git checkout test
#Do some changes inside the readme.txt file
Jim@local:~/webproject$ git commit -a -m 'edit readme'
Jim@local:~/webproject$ git checkout master
```

After performing a checkout on master, check the content of the `readme.txt` file. You will see that the content is the former content.

Playing with a branch

There are several commands useful for some features of branches. Firstly, you can easily rename a branch executing this:

```
Jim@local:~/webproject$ git branch -m old_name new_name
```

 To change the current branch, you can bypass the old_name variable:
`Jim@local:~/webproject$ git branch -m new_name`

Then, you can delete a branch:

```
Jim@local:~/webproject$ git branch -d test
```

You might get an error if there are uncommitted changes. You can force it:

```
Jim@local:~/webproject$ git branch -D test
```

Finally, you can push the changes of a branch to a remote repository.

While executing the `push` command, you can specify the remote branch to use:

```
Jim@local:~/webproject$ gitpush origin test
```

After performing a checkout on master, check the content of the `readme.txt` file. You will see that the content is the old one.

The difference between branches

To see the difference between two branches, you can execute this:

```
Jim@local:~/webproject$ git diff master test
```

Tracking branches

With Git, a branch can track another branch. This allows you to use the commands `pull` and `push`, without specifying the branch and repository.

For example, if you clone a Git repository, your local `master` branch is created as a tracking branch for the master branch of the origin repository.

To set up a tracking branch, execute this:

```
Jim@local:~/webproject$ git checkout -b new_branch origin/branch_to_track
#Or you can use this
Jim@local:~/webproject$ git branch new_branch origin/master
Jim@local:~/webproject$ git branch --track new_branch origin/master
```

Similarly, you can specify to not track a remote branch:

```
Jim@local:~/webproject$ git branch --no-track new_branch origin/master
#You can later update this branch and track origin/master
Jim@local:~/webproject$ git branch -u origin/master new_branch
```

Deleting a branch from the remote

Use this command if you want to delete a branch in the remote repository:

```
Erik@local:~/webproject$ git branch -d origin/test
```

Merging

A very nice process in Git allows you to combine the changes of two branches. This is called merging.

The `git merge` command performs a merge. You can merge changes from one branch to the current branch via the following command. Your local `master` branch is created as a tracking branch for the `master` branch of the `origin` repository:

```
Erik@local:~/webproject$ git checkout master
Erik@local:~/webproject$ git merge test
```

This command will merge test branch changes inside your current checked-out branch.

Fast forward merge

If the commits that are merged are direct predecessors of the HEAD pointer of the current branch, Git simplifies things by performing a so-called fast forward merge. This fast forward merge simply moves the HEAD pointer of the current branch to the last commit of the branch that is being merged.

This process is depicted in the following diagram. The first picture assumes that the master branch is checked out and you want to merge the changes of the branch labeled **branch** into your **master** branch. Each commit points to its predecessor (parent).

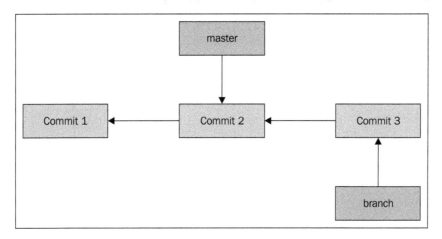

This diagram shows the current state of the repository. Now, we have to checkout to the master branch and merge the branch on it.

```
Erik@local:~/webproject$ git checkout master
Erik@local:~/webproject$ git merge branch
```

After the fast forward merge, the master branch will point to the last commit, as shown in the following diagram:

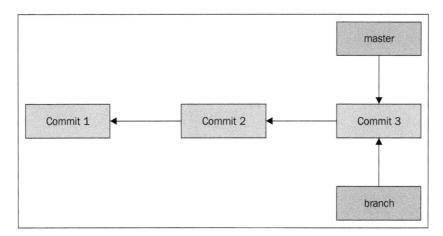

Merge commit

If commits are merged and are not from the same branch, it will lead to a three-way merge between the last commits of the two branches:

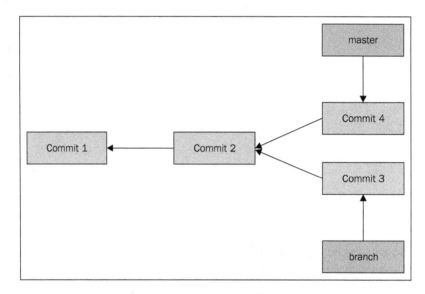

The result of this merge commit will be created on the current branch, with the changes of the last commit from both branches:

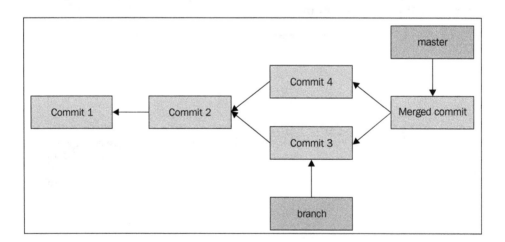

To use this strategy (without fast forward), you can use this command:

```
Erik@local:~/webproject$ git merge --no-ff
```

Other merging strategies

The merge command has certain parameters. You need to be certain as to when you will use them.

With the -s parameter, you can specify some merge strategies. There are two kinds of strategies; ours and theirs:

```
Erik@local:~/webproject$ git merge -s ours test
Erik@local:~/webproject$ git merge -s theirs test
```

The result of an ours strategy is that everything from the merged branch will be ignored. The theirs strategy will do the exact opposite.

For example, if we are try to push our modifications on index.html, and Git tells us that something is wrong because Jim pushed the useless changes on index.html earlier, you can apply the ours strategy, which will replace the changes made by Jim and use your file.

If Jim made the same changes that you made, but in a better way, you can apply the theirs strategy. It will remove your changes to use the file provided by Jim.

There is one strategy left; this is the recursive strategy. It allows you to specify the -x parameter to prefer your local/remote changes if there are conflicts from the two merged branches:

```
Erik@local:~/webproject$ git merge -s recursive -x ours test
Erik@local:~/webproject$ git merge -s recursive -x theirs test
```

 Be careful to not mix the ours or theirs strategy with the recursive strategy. The consequences will be different!

Rebase

As we just saw, the merge command combines the changes from two branches. The rebase command will take the changes from the first branch and apply them to the other branch.

In the rebase command do not merge commit!

The following diagram displays the current state of our repository. We have the **master** branch pointed on **Commit 3** and a branch pointed to **Commit 4**:

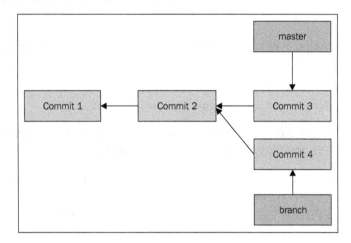

Our goal is to `rebase` branch from master, so we need to `checkout` on master and `rebase` it:

```
Erik@local:~/webproject$ git checkout branch
Erik@local:~/webproject$ git rebase master
```

The `rebase` command can be used if you want to get a feature (commits) from one branch to another and be sure to be close to the tip of the upstream branch. As we just saw, the command applies the changes from the branch called **branch** to the **master** branch.

In this schema, `commit 4` is applied on master by using the name `commit4bis`, and the original `commit 4` is deleted by the garbage collector.

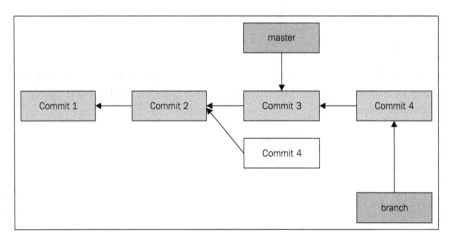

The --interactive option will stop after each commit to change messages, add files, or perform whatever else you want to.

There are some options for this command:

- Pick: This means that the commit is included
- Reword: This is similar to pick, and will let you alter the commit message
- Edit: This one will let you amend the commit
- Squash: This combines several commits into one
- Fixup: This is similar to Squash, without the possibility to change the commit message
- Exec: This lets you run the shell commands on a commit

 The merge command will create a new commit when merging two branches. The rebase command will apply the commits from one branch to another.

Cherry-pick

This command lets you select a commit from a branch to apply it to another. The patch will be considered as a new commit in the selected branch.

Let's try to understand this by exploring the following example: Jim creates the jim branch from master and adds a new file in it:

```
Jim@local:~/webproject$ git checkout -b jim
Jim@local:~/webproject$ touch home.html
Jim@local:~/webproject$ git add home.html
Jim@local:~/webproject$ git commit -m 'add homepage'
Jim@local:~/webproject$ echo "<html>...</html>" > home.html
Jim@local:~/webproject$ git commit -a -m 'add content inside home'
```

As you can see, Jim creates the home.html file, adds it into Git, and commits it. Then he edits it and commits again. Now, let's see the commit history for this branch:

```
Jim@local:~/webproject$ git log --oneline
4f6ec45 add content inside home
22c45b7 add homepage
```

Now, Jim will apply the first commit to the master branch:

```
Jim@local:~/webproject$ git checkout master
Jim@local:~/webproject$ git cherry-pick 22c45b7
```

Let's imagine that the cherry-pick went wrong and Jim wants to abort it:

```
Jim@local:~/webproject$ git cherry-pick --abort
```

However, if you want to roll back a cherry-pick, you have two ways to do it:

- If it's in a private branch, you can use the `git rebase` command
- If it's already in a public branch, use the `git revert` command

Using tags

Git has the option to tag a commit in the repository so that you find it easier. Most commonly, tags are used to mark an application version on a commit.

Creating and deleting tags

The command to create a tag is very easy:

```
Jim@local:~/webproject$ git tag 1.0.0
#Annotated tag contains a small description
Jim@local:~/webproject$ git tag 1.0.0 -m 'Release 1.0.0'
#Use a commit
Jim@local:~/webproject$ git tag 1.0.0 -m 'Release 1.0.0' commit_hash
```

Tags can also be deleted, but by default, it will only be inside your local repository. If you want to push the deleted one, you have to specify it. First, list all the available tags and delete the last tag:

```
Jim@local:~/webproject$ git tag
0.1.0
0.1.5
0.2.0
0.9.0
1.0.0
Jim@local:~/webproject$ git tag -l 0.1.*
0.1.0
0.1.5
Jim@local:~/webproject$ git tag -d 1.0.0
#Push it remotely
Jim@local:~/webproject$ git push origin tag 1.0.0
```

As I said earlier, tags are commonly used to mark a state of a release. They are called release tags.

By convention, the tag name will be `major_version.minor_version.patch_version`; for example, `1.0.0`.

> The patch version is incremented if there are backwards-compatible bug fixes.
>
> The minor version is incremented if there are bug fixes other than the backwards-compatible fix.
>
> The major version is incremented if there is at least one backward-incompatible bug fix.

After performing a check out on master, check the content of the `readme.txt` file. You will see that the content is the old one.

Summary

In this chapter, we saw how to work within a team using Git, which is very common for most developers. Now, you understand what a branch is, how we can merge them, and how to rebase one branch on another. We also saw how to tag a commit. Now you are ready to prepare and work on your Git repository, but there is something that has been left behind: what should you do if there are conflicts? The next chapter is dedicated to this question. We will see how to find something in your repository, explore the repository, and most importantly, how to fix conflicts and errors.

3

Finding and Resolving Conflicts

This chapter covers a part of Git that you will definitely meet: conflicts. How can we resolve them?

While working together as a team on a project, you will work on the same files. The `pull` command won't work because there are conflicts, and you might have tried some Git commands and things got bad. In this chapter, we will find solutions to these conflicts and see how we can fix them. We will cover the following topics:

- Finding content inside your Git repository
- Stashing your changes
- Fixing errors by practical examples

Finding content inside your repository

Sometimes, you will need to find something inside all your files. You can, of course, find it with the search feature of your OS, but Git already knows all your files.

Searching file content

To search text inside your files, simply use the following command:

```
Erik@server:~$ git grep "Something to find"
Erik@server:~$ git grep -n body
Master:Website.Index.html:4:          <bodyMaster:Website.Index.html:12:
</body>
```

It will display every match to the given keyword inside your code. All lines use the `[commitref]:[filepath]:[linenumber]:[matchingcontent]` pattern.

 Notice that `[commitref]` isn't displayed on all Git versions.

You can also specify the commit references that `grep` will use to search the keyword:

```
Erik@server:~$ git grep -n body d321f56 p88e03d HEAD~3
Master:Website.Index.html:4:          <body>
Master:Website.Index.html:12:         </body>
```

In this case, `grep` will look into the `d321f56`, `p88e03d`, and third commit starting by the head pointer.

 Your repository has to be encoded in UTF-8; otherwise, the `grep` command won't work.

Git allows you to use regex inside the search feature by replacing `somethingToFind` with a regex.

You can use the logical operators (`or` and `and`), as shown in the following command:

```
Erik@server:~$ git grep -e myRegex1 --or -e myRegex2
Erik@server:~$ git grep -e myRegex1 --and -e myRegex2
```

Let's see this with an example. We only have a `test.html` page inside our last commit, and we want to find whether or not there is a word with an uppercase alphabetic value and numeric values:

```
Erik@server:~$ git grep -e [A-Z] --and -e [0-9] HEAD
Master:Website.Test.html:6:          TEST01
```

With the `grep` command, you can delve deeper, but it's not necessary to discuss this topic here because you won't use it every day!

Showing the current status

The `git status` command is helpful if you have to analyze your repository:

```
Erik@server:~$ git status
# On branch master
# Your branch is ahead of 'origin/master' by 2 commits
```

```
# (use "git push" to publish your local commits)
# Changes not staged for commit:
#    (use "git add<file>..." to update what will be committed)
#    (use "git checkout -- <file>..." to discard changes in working
directory)
#
#   modified:    myFile1
#   modified:    myFile2
#
# Untracked files:
#    (use "git add<file>..." to include in what will be committed)
#
#   newFile.txt
no changes added to commit (use "git add" and/or "git commit -a")
```

Git analyzes the local repository in comparison to the remote repository. In this case, you have to add `newFile.txt`, commit `myFile1` and `myFile2`, and push them to the remote repository.

Exploring the repository history

The best way to explore the past commits inside your repository is to use the `git log` command. For this part, we will assume that there are only two commits.

To display all commits, use the following commands:

```
Erik@server:~$ git log --all
Commit xxxxxxxxxxx
Author: Jim <jim@mail.com>
Date: Sun Jul 20 15:10:12 2014 -0300
Fix front bugs on banner

Commit xxxxxxxxxxx
Author: Erik <erik@mail.com>
Date: Sat Jul 19 07:06:14 2014 -0300
Add the crop feature on website backend
```

This is probably not what you want. After several days of work, you will have plenty of these commits, so how will you filter it?

The power of the `git log` command is that you can quickly find anything in all commits.

Let's go for a quick overview of what Git is able to find. We will start by finding the last commit:

```
Erik@server:~$ git log -1
Commit xxxxxxxxxxx
Author: Jim <jim@mail.com>
Date: Sun Jul 20 15:10:12 2014 -0300
Fix front bugs on banner
```

The number after the `git log` command indicates that it is the first commit from `Head`.

Too easy! Let's try to find what the last commit of Erik is:

```
Erik@server:~$ git log --author=Erik -1
Commit xxxxxxxxxxx
Author: Erik <erik@mail.com>
Date: Sat Jul 19 07:06:14 2014 -0300
Add the crop feature on website backend
```

Now, let's find it between two dates:

```
Erik@server:~$ git log --author=Erik --before "2014-07-20" --after "2014-
07-18"
Commit xxxxxxxxxxx
Author: Erik <erik@mail.com>
Date: Sat Jul 19 07:06:14 2014 -0300
Add the crop feature on website backend
```

As I told you earlier, there are a lot of parameters to the `git log` command. You can see all of them using the `git help log` command.

The `stat` parameter is really useful:

```
Erik@server:~$ git log --author=Jim --stat
Commit xxxxxxxxxxx
Author: Jim <jim@mail.com>
Date: Sun Jul 20 15:10:12 2014 -0300
Fix front bugs on banner
```

```
index.php | 1 +
        1 file changed, 1 insertion(+)
```

This parameter allows you to view a summary of the changes made in each commit. If you want to see the full changes, try the -p parameter.

Remember that the git log command has a file parameter to restrict the search to the git log [file] file.

Viewing changes

There are two ways to see changes in a repository: git diff and git show.

The git diff command lets you see the changes that are not committed. For example, we have an index.php file and replace the file content by a line. Just before the lines, you will see a plus (+) or minus (-) sign. The + sign means that content was added and the – sign denotes that it was removed:

```
Erik@server:~$ git diff
diff --git a/index.php b/index.php
indexb4d22ea..748ebb2 100644
--- a/index.php
+++ b/index.php
@@ -1,11 +1 @@
-<html>
-
-<head>
-<title>Git is great!</title>
-</head>
-<body>
-<?php
- echo 'Git is great';
-?>
-</body>
-</html>
+<b> I added a line</b>
```

If you want to analyze a commit, I suggest you to use the `git show` command. It will display the full list of changes of the commit:

```
Erik@server:~$ git show commitId
```

There is a way to do the opposite, that is, to display commits for a file with `git blame`:

```
Erik@server:~$ git blameindex.php
e4bac680 (Erik 2014-07-20 19:00:47 +0200 1) <b> I added a line</b>
```

Stashing your changes

Git has a command that allows you to save the current state of the local working repository and go back to the last committed revision with `git stash`.

This is really helpful when you have to develop an urgent fix. After this, you can restore the stashed changes and continue with your development.

To use this command, just execute the following command snippet:

```
Erik@server:~$ git stash
#Do your fix and then unstash edit
Erik@server:~$ git stash pop
```

Of course, you can do more with this command, such as save a list of stashes:

```
Erik@server:~$ git stash
#See the list of available stashes
Erik@server:~$ git stash list
#Apply the second stash
Erik@server:~$ git stash apply stash@"1}
#Delete a stash
Erik@server:~$ git stash drop stash@"1}
#Or delete all stashes
Erik@server:~$ git stash clear
```

Let's suppose that your stash concerns a feature and you haven't created a dedicated branch for it. You can simply create a branch executing this command:

```
Erik@server:~$ git stash branch mynewbranchname
```

Remember this command is only for urgent fixes. If you want to add a new feature, you should use a new branch.

Cleaning your mistakes

The first thing to know is that you can always clean your mistake with Git. Sometimes this will be hard or painful for your code, but you can do it!

Let's start this section with how to remove untracked files:

```
Erik@server:~$ git clean -n
```

The -n option will make a dry-run (it's always important to see what will happen before you regret it).

If you want to also remove directories and hidden files, use this one:

```
Erik@server:~$ git clean -fdx
```

With these options, you will delete new directories (-d) and hidden files (-x) and be able to force them (-f).

Reverting uncommitted changes

To explain this section, we will use an example. Let's suppose you edited a file on the production working directory, but didn't commit it. On your last push, you edited it, and the changes in production aren't needed anymore. So, your goal is to erase changes on this file and reset the file to the last committed version:

```
Erik@server:~$ git checkout the_filename
```

This command is really nice if you want to restore a deleted file. You can also specify a commit pointer to use (useful if you stash your changes):

```
Erik@server:~$ rm myfile.txt
Erik@server:~$ git checkout HEAD myfile.txt
```

The git reset command

The git reset command will allow you to go back to a previous state (for example, commit). The git reset command has three options (soft, hard, or mixed, by default).

In general, the git reset command's aim is to take the current branch, reset it to point somewhere else, and possibly bring the index and work tree along. More concretely, if the master branch (currently checked out) looks like the first row (in the following figure) and you want it to point to B and not C, you will use this command:

```
Erik@server:~$ git reset B
```

The following diagram shows exactly what happened with the previous command. The HEAD pointer was reset from C to B:

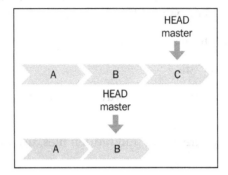

The following table explains what the options really move:

Option	Head pointer	Working tree	Staging area
Soft	Yes	No	No
Mixed	Yes	No	Yes
Hard	Yes	Yes	Yes

The three options that you can provide on the reset command can be easily explained:

- --hard: This option is the simplest. It will restore the content to the given commit. All the local changes will be erased. The git reset --hard command means git reset --hard HEAD, which will reset your files to the previous version and erase your local changes.

- --mixed: This option resets the index, but not the work tree. It will reset your local files, but the differences found during the process will be marked as local modifications if you analyze them using git status. It's very helpful if you make some bugs on previous commits and want to keep your local changes.

- --soft: This option will keep all your files, such as mixed, intact. If you use git status, it will appear as changes to commit. You can use this option when you have not committed files as expected, but your work is correct. So you just have to recommit it the way you want.

The git reset command doesn't remove untracked files; use git clean instead.

Editing a commit

There are several tricks to edit your last commit.

If you want to edit the description of your last commit, use the following line:

```
Erik@server:~$ git commit --amend
```

Let's suppose that your last commit contains buggy code; you can specify that your changes on the file are part of the last commit:

```
Erik@server:~$ git add filename.txt
Erik@server:~$ git commit -v -amend
```

Now I want to remove a file I included accidentally in the last commit (because this file deserves a new commit):

```
Erik@server:~$ git reset HEAD^1 filename.txt
Erik@server:~$ git commit --amend -v
Erik@server:~$ git commit -v filename.txt
```

You might ask yourself what the HEAD^ and HEAD~ notations are.

It is just a shorthand to specify commits without using the commit ID.

HEAD~ is short for HEAD~1 and is the commit's first parent. HEAD~2 stands for the commit's grandparents.

HEAD^ also refers to the commit's first parent.

Of course, you can use them together, such as HEAD~3^2, which means the commit's second generation ancestor of HEAD. Let's check the following scheme to clearly understand it:

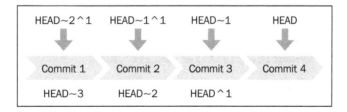

Canceling a commit

The `git revert` command allows you to "cancel" your last unpushed commit. I used quotes around cancel because Git doesn't drop the commit; it creates a new commit that executes the opposite of your commit. A pushed commit is irreversible, so you cannot change it.

Firstly, let's have a look at the last commits:

```
Erik@server:~$ git log
commite4bac680c5818c70ced1205cfc46545d48ae687e
Author: Eric Pidoux
Date:   Sun Jul 20 19:00:47 2014 +0200
replace all
commit0335a5f13b937e8367eff35d78c259cf2c4d10f7
Author: Eric Pidoux
Date:   Sun Jul 20 18:23:06 2014 +0200
commitindex.php
```

We want to cancel the `0335`... commit:

```
Erik@server:~$ git revert 0335a5f13
```

Canceling this commit isn't necessary to enter the full commit ID, but just the first characters. Git will find it, but you will have to enter at least six characters to be sure that there isn't another commit that starts with the same characters.

Rewriting commit history

Sometimes a situation will occur where you want to remove a file from all commits because it contains confidential information. You can do it by using `git filter-branch`:

```
Erik@server:~$ git filter-branch --index-filter 'git rm --cached
--ignore-unmatch myconfidentialfilename.txt' HEAD
```

I used the `-ignore-unmatch` option because `gitrm` will fail if the file is absent from the tree.

Solving merge conflicts

When you are working with several branches, a conflict will probably occur while merging them. It appears if two commits from different branches modify the same content and Git isn't able to merge them.

If it occurs, Git will mark the conflict and you have to resolve it.

For example, Jim modified the `index.html` file on a feature branch and Erik has to edit it on another branch. When Erik merges the two branches, the conflict occurs.

Git will tell you to edit the file to resolve the conflict. In this file, you will find the following:

```
<<<<<<< HEAD
Changes from Erik
=======
Changes from Jim
>>>>>>> b2919weg63bfd125627gre1911c8b08127c85f8
```

The `<<<<<<<` characters indicate the start of the merge conflict, the `======` characters indicate the break points used for comparison, and `>>>>>>>` indicate the end of the conflict.

To resolve a conflict, you have to analyze the differences between the two changes and merge them manually. Don't forget to delete the signs added by Git. After resolving it, simply commit the changes.

If your merge conflict is too complicated to resolve because you can't easily find the differences, Git provides a useful tool to help you.

Git's `diff` helps you to find differences:

```
Diff --git erik/mergetestjim/mergetest
Index.html 88h3d45..92f62w 130634
--- erik/mergetest
+++ jim/mergetest
@@ -1,3 +1,4 @@
<body>
+I added this code between
This is the file content
-I added a third line of code
+And this is the last one
```

So, what happened? The command displays some lines with the changes, with the + mark coming from `origin/master`; those marked with – are from your local repository, and of course, the lines without a mark are common to both repositories.

Searching errors with git bisect

The `git bisect` command allows you to run a binary search through the commit history to find a commit that has an issue.

For example, you pulled the last commits and the website isn't working anymore. You know that before the last pull everything was okay! So you have to find the commit ID before it crashes and the last ID after the pull:

```
Erik@server:~$ git bisect start
Erik@server:~$ git bisect bad commitIDAfterThePull
Erik@server:~$ git bisect good commitIDBefore
```

Now, the bisecting loop begins and Git will check for an alternative commit. Reset the given commit and tell Git whether the website is working:

```
Erik@server:~$git bisect badcommitID
```

Git will search again and again to find which commit crashed the website:

```
Erik@server:~$ git show theCommitID
```

Here we are! Instead of trying to locate a bug inside all your files, you have a shortened list of files.

If you don't want to reset to a given commit and test the website, you can create a bash script and tell Git to use it. The script has to return 0 if the condition is fulfilled, and nonzero if it isn't.

For example, we want to check the existence of a file:

```
#!/bin/bash
FILE=$1
If [ -f $FILE];
Then
  Exit 0;
Else
  Exit 1;
fi
```

Now it's time to run `git bisect` to specify the last 10 commits:

```
Erik@server:~$ git bisect start HEAD HEAD~10
Erik@server:~$ git bisect run ./check_file.sh index.html
```

The algorithm used by `git bisect` always returns the commit that is at the middle position of the array.

In the following diagram, you will see how the algorithm found the good commit in three steps:

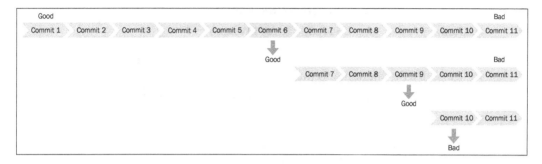

The **Commit6** option is selected by Git. After checking it, you tell Git that it's good.

Git reduces the array because if **Commit6** is good, then every commit between **Commit1** and **Commit6** is good too.

Then Git asks you to test **Commit9**, and you say that it's good too.

So the error can only be inside **Commit10** and **Commit11**.

Fixing errors by practical examples

This section will help the readers a lot because the errors mentioned can occur very frequently. This will summarize the entire chapter. Sometimes, especially when you are not really familiar with Git, you don't know how to fix it. Here are the most common errors that will occur:

- **Remote origin already exists**: This error occurs when you already have a remote repository specified and the remote origin removed and added:

    ```
    Erik@server:~$ git remote rm origin
    Erik@server:~$ git remote add origin https://github.com/sexyboys/
    InflexibleBundle.git
    ```

- **Git push fails with rejected error**: This error occurs because you didn't execute `git pull` before `git push`:

    ```
    Erik@server:~$ git pull
    Erik@server:~$ git push
    ```

- **Git push fails with "fatal: The remote end hung up unexpectedly"**: This one is common and you should check whether your remote URL is correct and Git has access to the remote repository.

- **Restoring a changed file to its last committed state**: Run `git checkout` followed by the filename and you will lose your changes. However, this will be restored as a clean copy of the file:

```
Erik@server:~$ git checkout theFilename
```

- **Unstaging a file**: Did you run `git add` too soon? Run `git reset HEAD` followed by the filename to unstage it:

```
Erik@server:~$ git reset HEAD theFilename
```

- **How to fix the most recent commit message?**

   The `-amend` option will edit a commit message:

```
Erik@server:~$ git commit --amend
```

   The editor will open to edit the last message.

- **Reset the most recent commit**: There are two ways to do this: with and without your changes.

   ◦ Without losing changes:

```
Erik@server:~$ git reset HEAD~1
```

   ◦ By losing changes:

```
Erik@server:~$ git reset --hard HEAD~1
```

- **I found a bug after releasing the product but it was in the commit that I did a long time ago, how to fix it?**: In this case, you should not use `git reset` because it rewrites the history and the product is already released. Therefore, you should make a commit that reverts the buggy commit and pushes it to share with your colleagues:

```
Erik@server:~$ git revert theCommitID
```

- **There are many garbage files in the working directory. How to delete them?**: In this situation, the files are not maintained by Git, so you have to use `git clean`:

```
#To check the files that will be removed
Erik@server:~$ git clean -n
#Removethem
Erik@server:~$ git clean -f
```

- **I think I made a mistake while resolving conflicted files. How do I restore it to the state just after git merge?**: To do this, you can use `git checkout`:

  `Erik@server:~$ git checkout --merge theFilename`

- **Gitindex file is corrupt**: No need to worry. This one is rare but can be annoying! Git will display the error as `bad index file sha1 signature`:

  `fatal: index file corrupt`

  You just have to remove the backup index file; remove it, and then reset the repository:

  `Erik@server:~$ mv .git/index .git/indexOLD`

  `Erik@server:~$ git reset`

- **Git refuses to start a merge/pull command**: The typical error messages look like this:

  - **Error**: The `index.html` entry is not up to date; it cannot be merged
  - **Error**: The `index.html` entry will be overwritten by the `merge` command

  To resolve this, perform the following steps:

  1. Stash the changes or throw them out:

     `Erik@server:~$ git stash save "my message"`

     `Erik@server:~$ git checkout index.html`

  2. Check that the changes are staged:

     `Erik@server:~$ git status`

  3. Bring the changes from the remote repository:

     `Erik@server:~$ git pull`

  4. Repopulate if you made a stash:

     `Erik@server:~$ git stash pop`

Summary

In this chapter, we saw how to find something inside your Git repository and resolve mistakes. Now, you should not be afraid to make some mistakes because you know that you can repair them. At the end of this chapter, we saw the most common errors that occur.

For the next chapter, you will learn to delve deeper into Git and overview all the possibilities with the versioning system.

4
Going Deeper into Git

We have seen the most common features of Git, but we did not cover everything. The aim of this chapter is to discuss features that can help, but are not absolutely essential:

- Migrating an SVN repository to Git
- Using Git within an SVN environment
- Managing Git submodules
- Creating and applying patches
- Git hooks

Migrating an SVN repository to Git

Companies are afraid to change their versioning systems. They often try to explain themselves by saying that Git is too complicated, it has insufficient features, or even both.

Git is not necessarily better than **Subversion** (**SVN**), it's just different. For example, if you are developing on the road with SVN, you cannot commit your changes if the repository can't be reached. Git is decentralized, so your local working copy is a repository. Git is a bit harder to learn than SVN, but it adds complexities such as two modes to create repositories, a checkout/clone, a commit/push, and so on.

In one word, Git is more flexible. There is more than one way to do a task. Also, its backbone is its community that develops ingenious tools (GitHub, add-ons inside editors, and GitLab).

SVN to Git migration is extremely simple, and we can retain the repository's entire history. This is not a sufficient reason to not migrate your repositories. If you want to use Git, you can do so even if you already use SVN.

We will see the migration process in a few easy-to-follow steps.

Preparing for SVN to Git migration

Firstly, we want to keep the users; so, we have to create a text file that displays the mapping between SVN users and Git users.

To do this, create a text file inside the svn repository, and call it `authors.txt`:

```
Erik@server:~/svn$ nano authors.txt
Erik@server:~/svn$ svn log ^/ --xml | grep -P "^<author" | sort -u | \
    perl -pe 's/<author>(.*?)<\/author>/$1 = /' > authors.txt
```

Now you have a text file that includes all SVN users, one per line. Edit this text file and map the SVN users with the Git users. For example, consider the following:

```
eriksvn = Erik <erik@mymail.com>
jimsvn = Jim <jim@mymail.com>
```

Copy this file into the future Git repository, and we are ready to migrate:

```
Erik@server:~/git$ cp ../svn/authors.txt authors.txt
```

 The Git directory I used isn't initialized, it's just an empty directory.

Migrating from SVN to Git

The `git svn` command will help us to migrate from one repository to another. To use this command, just type the following:

```
Erik@server:~/git$ git svn clone svn://mySvnRepositoryPATH --authors-
file=authors.txt
Initialized empty Git repository in /home/erik/git/myRepoName/.git/
...
```

This command displays what it is doing, so you just have to wait. So, go take a beer/coffee while it's running!

We now have a Git repository with the full history of the previous commit. If you wish to check it out, execute the `git log` command:

```
Erik@server:~/git/myRepoName$ git log
commit df9448ff53864d8cfc6f78fd8831fd363d63a28b
Author: Erik <erik@mymail.com>
Date:   Thu July 10 06:44:47 2014 +0000
```

```
Change the header

    git-svn-id: svn://mySvnRepository@48121 ac52e18a-acf5-0310-9fe8-
c4428f23b10a


commit 7e126efa063a1ed3203225efe973adb9286aa803
Author: Jim <jim@mymail.com>
Date:     Wed July 9 21:53:52 2014 +0000

    Fix slider on homepage

    git-svn-id: svn://mySvnRepository@47970 ac52e18a-acf5-0310-9fe8-
c4428f23b10a
```

Cleaning your commits

We just saw that Git added a short reference to the SVN commit on the `git commit` messages. If you want to remove these references, you can use the `git filter-branch` command:

```
Erik@server:~/git/myRepoName$ git filter-branch -msg-filter '
        sed -e "/git-svn-id:/d"'
```

This command will clean your entire commit message by removing the short references added by the `git svn` command.

Pushing content on Git

Now it's time to add the remote repository and push the content on it:

```
Erik@server:~/git/myRepoName$ git remote add origin ssh://myRemotePath/
myRemoteRepository.git
```

Migrating branches and tags

We have seen the easiest way to migrate a repository. There is also a way to migrate the branches and tags. To do this, add these options to the `git svn` command line:

```
Erik@server:~/ $ git svn clone --authors-file=authors.txt svn://
myRepositoryPath --trunk=trunk --branches=branches --tags=tags
```

In fact, we specified to Git where the trunk, branch, and tag directories are, and where to migrate them to. The migration is, of course, longer.

Now, we have to track the directories because if you list the imported branches, you will see this result:

```
Erik@server:~/git/myRepoName$ git branch -a
* master
  Remotes/myBranch1
  Remotes/myBranch2
  Remotes/tags/myBranch2_1@2249
  Remotes/trunk
```

All branches and tags are tracked remotely, so we have to recreate them locally:

```
Erik@server:~/git/myRepoName$ git branch myBranch1 remotes/myBranch1
Erik@server:~/git/myRepoName$ git branch -l
myBranch1
* master
Erik@server:~/git/myRepoName$ git branch myBranch2_1 remotes/tags/
myBranch2_1@2249
Erik@server:~/git/myRepoName$ git tag -l
myBranch2_1
```

When we recreate all branches and tags locally, we push them remotely:

```
Erik@server:~/git/myRepoName$ git push -u origin master
Erik@server:~/git/myRepoName$ git push --all
Erik@server:~/git/myRepoName$ git push --tags
```

Another easy way to migrate

GitHub provides its own tool to migrate. For more information, go to `https://porter.github.com/new`.

It helps you to migrate your repository easily in a few steps:

1. Type the URL of the project you want to import and check out this URL.
2. Provide the GitHub user that will own the repository and the name of your repository after migration.
3. Choose whether this will be a public or private repository.
4. Click on **Begin Import**.

This is all! Of course, you have less configuration possibilities than the ones mentioned earlier (authors, commits, and so on), but it is a quick way to migrate.

Using Git within an SVN environment

If you want to use Git as your versioning system, you shouldn't only migrate every repository from SVN to Git, but you should also use Git locally. The `Git-svn` command will help you do this. It so happens that your team doesn't want to change its versioning system, or a project is way too big to migrate on a new versioning system. So, Git has a solution for you; how about using Git features without anyone knowing or caring?

The following diagram explains how to use Git inside an SVN environment. When executing a Git command, the SVN environment will not notice it because the `Git-svn` command will convert all your commands.

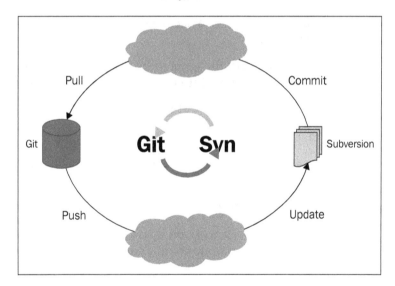

Setting up your repository

We assume that you already have an SVN repository and you want to use Git locally. As a first step, clone the SVN repository using this command:

```
Erik@server:~$ git svn clone -s http://my_website.com/my_subversion_repo
my_gitsvn_local
```

The -s option stands for standard layout, which means that your subversion layout has three directories (trunk, branches, and tags). You can, of course, forget this option if your repository does not have a standard layout.

This creates a Git repository under the my_gitsvn_local directory that is mapped to the trunk folder of your subversion repository.

> As Git doesn't track empty directories, the empty directories under the trunk won't appear inside your Git repository.

Sometimes you might have to clone a big repository. In this case, checking out the commit history will be lengthy because the repository is too big. There is a way to clone it without waiting for a long time.

You can do this by cloning the repository with the earlier version of the repository:

```
Erik@server:~$ git svn clone -s -r500:HEAD http://my_website.com/my_
subversion_repo my_gitsvn_local
```

There is one last thing to set up. Every file ignored by SVN has to be ignored by Git too. To do this, you have to transfer them into the .gitignore file by using this:

```
Erik@server:~$ git svn show-ignore > .gitignore
```

There is an alternative method that uses the update-index command:

```
Erik@server:~$ git update-index --assume-unchanged filesToIgnore
```

Working with Git SVN

Once your repository is ready, you can work on it and start executing Git commands as we saw earlier. Of course, there are some commands to execute when you want to push or pull from the SVN repository. When you want to update your local Git repository, just type this:

```
Erik@server:~$ git svn rebase
```

To commit back to SVN, use the following command:

```
Erik@server:~$ git svn dcommit
```

Sooner or later, you will add the .svn folder to the staging area in Git. Hopefully, there is a way to delete it:

```
Erik@server:~$ git status -s | grep .svn | awk "'print $3'} | xargs git
rm -cached
```

Managing Git submodules

You will probably work on a project that requires dependency on another project. This can be a library that was developed by you or another team. It can be hard to manage when the library is updated and you made some custom code inside your project.

Git handles this by using submodules. It allows you to manage a Git repository as a subfolder of another Git repository, which in turn lets you clone a repository isolated from the commits of the current repository.

Adding a submodule

Let's imagine you are working on a website and you want to add the fpdf library that helps you create a PDF file in PHP. The first thing to do is to clone the library's Git repository inside your subfolder:

```
Erik@server:~/mySite/$ git submodule add https://github.com/lsolesen/
fpdf.git fpdf
Cloning in 'fpdf'
remote: Counting objects: 966, done.
remote: Total 966 (delta 0), reused 0 (delta 0)
Receiving objects: 100% (966/966), 5.96 MiB | 1.13 MiB/s, done.
Resolving deltas: 100% (292/292), done.
```

You now have the Fpdf project inside the fpdf folder. You can do everything you want inside it, such as add modifications, change the remote repository, push your changes in the remote repository, and so on.

While you add the Git submodule, Git adds two files, Fpdf and .gitmodules. Let's see this with the git status command:

```
Erik@server:~/mySite/$ git status
# On branch master
# Changes to be committed:
#   (use "git reset HEAD <file>…" to unstage)
#     new file: .gitmodules
#     new file: Fpdf
```

If you display a .gitmodules file using the cat command, you will find all the submodules entitled as follows:

- Fpdf: This is the folder where the repository is located
- .gitmodules: This is a config file that saves the link between the submodule you just added and the project URL:
  - Erik@server:~/mySite/$ cat .gitmodules
  - [submodule "Fpdf"]
- path: This is given as fpdf
- url: This is given as https://github.com/lsolesen/fpdf.git
- .gitmodules: If you have several submodules, you will have the preceding entry for every submodule inside this file

 Git sees the fpdf folder as a submodule, so it won't track the changes if you're not in this folder. An important fact is that Git saves this addition as a nonregular commit of this repository, so if someone clones your website, Git can recreate the same environment.

Cloning a project with submodules

If you clone a project using submodules (as shown in the previous example), Git will add all files other than the submodule files:

```
Erik@server:~$ git clone git://theurl.com/mySite.git
Initialized empty Git repository in /var/www/mySite/.git/
remote: Counting objects: 6, done.
remote: Compressing objects: 100% (4/4), done.
remote: Total 6 (delta 0), reused 0 (delta 0)
Receiving objects: 100% (6/6), done.
$ cd mySite
$ ls -l
total 8
-rw-r--r--   1 epidoux   admin    3 Aug   19 10:24 index.html
drwxr-xr-x  2 epidoux   admin   68 Aug   19 10:24 fpdf
```

The fpdf folder is created, but it is empty. You will have to execute these two commands to initialize the import submodule:

```
Erik@server:~$ git submodule init
Submodule 'fpdf' (git://github.com/lsolesen/fpdf.git) registered for path
'fpdf'
```

```
Erik@server:~$ git submodule update
Initialized empty Git repository in /var/www/mySite/fpdf/.git/
...
```

Your repository is now up to date. Using submodules can be interesting if you want to separate and isolate some parts of your code.

 If you execute a `git pull` command on your project, you will not have the last version of the submodule. To do this, you have to execute `git submodule update` every time you want to update your submodule.

Removing a submodule

To remove a submodule from your project, you have to execute these steps:

1. Delete the lines of the submodule from the `.gitmodules` file.
2. Delete the submodule part from `.git/config`.
3. Delete the submodule from Git by executing this command:

   ```
   Erik@server:~$ git rm -cached submodule_path
   ```

4. Commit and delete the untracked files.

Using a subtree instead of a submodule

There are a lot of articles on the Internet that explain why you should not use Git modules. In these articles, they point to the fact that you have to use `git submodule update` every time, and you will probably forget to do this.

The second problem is that Git doesn't really handle merging into a submodule. It detects SHA conflicts, but this is all. It's left to you to find out what should be done.

Thankfully, there is the subtree, which is better in a few ways:

- Easy to manage for light workflow
- While you clone a superproject, the subproject's code is available too
- Subtree doesn't use files such as `.gitmodules`
- The most important point is that contents can be modified inside your project without having a copy of the dependency elsewhere

`Git subtree` is available from Version 1.7.11 (May 2012) of Git.

Now, we will see how to add and manage a subtree in the following section.

Adding a subproject with a subtree

Firstly, we need to tell Git that we want to include a project as a subtree. We use the `git remote` command to specify where the remote repository of this subtree is:

```
Erik@server:~$ git remote add -f fpdf_remote git://github.com/lsolesen/
fpdf.git
```

Now, you can add the subtree inside your project using the remote repository:

```
Erik@server:~$ git subtree add --prefix fpdf fpdf_remote master --squash
```

This will create the subproject. If you want to update it later, you will have to use the `fetch` and `subtree pull` commands:

```
Erik@server:~$ git fetch fpdf_remote master
Erik@server:~$ git subtree pull fpdf fpdf_remote master --squash
```

Contributing on a subtree

Obviously, you can commit your fixes to the subproject in the local directory, but when you push back upstream, you will have to use another remote repository:

```
Erik@server:~$ git remote add epidoux-fpdf ssh://git@github.com/epidoux/
fpdf.git
Erik@server:~$ git subtree push --prefix=fpdf epidoux-fpdf master
Git push using: epidoux-fpdf master
Counting objects: 1, done.
Delta compression using up to 1 thread.
Compressing objects: 100% (1/1), done.
Writing objects: 100% (1/1), 150 bytes, done.
Total 1 (delta 1), reused 0 (delta 0)
To ssh://git@github.com/epidoux/fpdf.git
   243ab46..dca35db dbca35db 21fe51c9b5824370b3b224c440b3470cb -} master
```

`Git subtree` can be an easy way if you have to frequently update your subproject and want to contribute to it with less effort.

Creating and applying patches

A patch is a piece of code that can apply a set of changes (that is, a commit) to any branch and any order of a project. The main goal of this feature is to share the changes with other developers, and it gives control to the project maintainer (whether they choose to incorporate the contribution or not). Creating a patch in Git is very easy, as we will see right now.

Creating a patch

Creating a Git format patch will include metadata on the specified commit (author, message, and so on). Everything will be formatted as an easy-to-send e-mail. So, the recipient of this patch will be able to recreate the commit with `git am`.

In fact, the `git format-patch` command is useful to transfer a commit. Otherwise, the `git diff` command finds differences inside the code.

In cases where we want to create a patch for one commit, we have to add the `sha1` code of the commit.

The `git log` command, as we saw in *Chapter 2, Working in a Team Using Git*, shows the commits:

```
Erik@server:~$ git log --pretty=oneline -5
```

Now, we have the `commit` key to create the patch:

```
Erik@server:~$ git format-patch -1 theSha1 --stdout > myPatch.patch
```

When we get the patch generated by `git-format`, we can read metadata to know what the patch is for. There are two important options:

- The `stat` option lists the difference statuses on the standard output:
  ```
  Erik@server:~$ git apply --stat myPatch.patch
  ```

- The `check` option tells us whether the patch can be applied:
  ```
  Erik@server:~$ git apply --check myPatch.patch
  ```

For example, let's say Erik wants to change the title of the `index.html` file. He has no write access to the remote repository. He edits the file and commits his change. So, his file looks like this:

```
<html>
  <head>
    <title>Erik new title</title>
  </head>
```

```
<body>

</body>
</html>
```

Now that the file is edited, we can commit the change and generate a patch:

Erik@server:~$ git commit -a -m "Change the title"

Erik@server:~$ git format-patch master

 Using the format-patch command with the branch name tells Git
to generate patches for each commit in the current branch that are
missing from the master branch.

The last command will create a file called 0001-Change-the-title. If you open the
generated patch file, you will find something like this:

```
Index 98e10a1..854cc34 100643
--- a/index.html
+++ b/index.html
@@ -3,4 +3,3 @@
  <head>
-   <title> The old common title </title>
+   <title>Erik new title</title>
  </head>
```

You will quickly notice that the patch contains your last commit on changing
the title.

Mailing the patch

In the previous section, we saw an example where Erik changes the title of our
index.html page and creates a patch with the change. Now, he wants to send it to
the project maintainer because his title is much more interesting than the previous
one. There are three methods to send an e-mail with a patch:

- Copy and paste the content of the patch into an e-mail
- Attach the patch file to an e-mail
- Use the git send-email command

Applying the patch

Jim is the maintainer of this project and decided to apply the patch made by Erik. You have to move to the right repository, and after you check the patch that is applicable, you just have to use the `git am` command with the `signoff` option. This option will use the identity metadata from the patch, and not your metadata. You can use the `k` option too, which keeps the flags:

```
Jim@local:~$ git checkout -b patch-branch
Jim@local:~$ git am --signoff -k < 001-Change-the-title.patch
```

Jim checks out a new topic branch called **patch-branch** to test the patch without destroying the project features. With the `git am` command, Jim creates a new commit with the patch change.

 In our example, Jim integrates the change in the same order as Erik, but it didn't have to be like this. The idea of the patch feature is to isolate a commit and integrate it when you want.

Git hooks

Git has a way to execute scripts when a Git command is performed. It will help you to perform some automated actions while you or one of your team members executes a Git command. The uses of these scripts are unlimited and very easy to set up. It will be very helpful to get notifications, format code, deploy websites, perform tasks on folders, and so on.

There are two types of hooks, depending on the commands:

* **Client hooks**: These kinds of hooks are for client operations, such as the `commit` or `merge` command

* **Server hooks**: These hooks are for Git server-side operations, such as the `push` command

Client hooks

There are many types of hooks for the client side; we choose to present the two most-known kinds. The first hook, `pre-commit`, works with the committing process. Firstly, the `pre-commit` hook is run before typing a commit message. It is used to inspect what you will commit, and it will be interesting to inspect your code to check that you forget nothing.

The commit is aborted if your script exits with a nonzero value. It is a pretty handful way to check if there are documentations on new methods.

The second hook is the `prepare-commit-msg` hook. The `prepare-commit-msg` hook is run after the default message is created. It will be useful to manage autogenerated messages for merge and amended commits.

Server hooks

Server hooks are run before and after interactions with the server. As seen previously, a nonzero value rejects the push. It is used to enforce the policy of your repository.

When pushing commits, the first script that should be run is `pre-receive`. You can use it to check that the user has enough permission to push.

The `post-receive` hook runs after the entire process is complete and is mainly used to notify other services or users. This script won't stop the push; it is only there to notify.

The third script to run is `update`, which is pretty close to the `pre-receive` script, except that it runs for each updating branch.

After the entire commit process is completed, the `post-commit` hook runs. It is used for notifications only.

More about hooks

As hooks can help you a lot with repetitive tasks, you will find a quick summary of the most well-known hooks in the following table:

Hook	Type	Trigger	Can reject?
pre-commit	Client	Before the commit	Yes, the commit
post-commit	Client	After the commit	No
commit-msg	Client	During the commit	No
update	Server	While receiving the push	Yes, the push
pre-receive	Server	Before a receive pack	Yes
post-receive	Server	After a receive pack	No
post-update	Server	During a push from the client side	No
post-checkout	Client	After a checkout	No
post-merge	Client	After a merge	No

All types of hooks come with environment variables that are available inside your hook. The following is a list of variables for each hook and more information about how to use them:

- `applypatch-msg`, `post-applypatch`, and `pre-applypatch`: These three hooks can only be used in a working tree; they contain the following environment variables:
    - ° `GIT_AUTHOR_DATE` (for example, `'Wed, 5 November, 2014 10:40:22 +0200'`)
    - ° `GIT_AUTHOR_NAME` (for example, `'Erik'`)
    - ° `GIT_AUTHOR_EMAIL` (for example, `'erik@localhost'`)
    - ° `GIT_REFLOG_ACTION` (the command that trigged the hook, for example, `'am'`)
    - ° `GIT_DIR`, which is not set

- `pre-commit`, `prepare-commit-msg`, `commit-msg`, and `post-commit`: Similar to the previous hooks, these work in a working tree and there are less variables:
    - ° `GIT_DIR` is set to `'.git'`
    - ° `GIT_INDEX_FILE` is set to `'.git/index'`

- `post-checkout`: This hook can only be used in a working tree too. The variables include:
    - ° `GIT_DIR`, which is set to `'.'`

- `pre-receive`, `update`, `post-receive`, and `post-update`: These last ones can be run in a bare or nonbare repository, and there is only one environment variable set:
    - ° `GIT_DIR`, which is set to `'.'`

Installing a hook

Hooks are stored in the hooks subfolder of the Git repository, `.git/hooks`.

By default, Git provides some examples in this directory. You can write the scripts in Perl, Python, Ruby, PHP, and so on (executable script only).

When you want to create a hook, put the file inside the hooks folder and check the execution permissions.

A hook example

Let's build an example using the post-receive hook; we will deploy a website using no more than the hook. We assume that the remote Git repository and running site are on the same server.

First, add a script inside .git/hooks:

```
Erik@server :~/mySite$ git nano .git/post-receive
#!/bin/sh
#
## store the arguments
read oldrev newrev refname

## define the log file
LOGFILE=./post-receive.log

# The running site
DEPLOYDIR=/var/www/html/mySite

# The maintenance htaccess file
MAINTENANCE=.htaccess_maintenance

##  Record the push
echo -e "Incoming Push at $( date +%F )" >> $LOGFILE
echo " - Old SHA: $oldrev New SHA: $newrev Branch Name: $refname" >>
$LOGFILE

## Update the deployed copy
echo "Deploying..." >> $LOGFILE

echo " - Entering the maintenance mode "
cd /var/www/html/mySite
mv .htaccess .htaccess_prod
mv $MAINTENANCE .htaccess
echo " - Updating code"
GIT_WORK_TREE="$DEPLOYDIR" git checkout -f
```

```
echo " - Exiting maintenance mode"
mv .htaccess $MAINTENANCE
mv .htaccess_prod .htaccess
```

```
echo "Finished Deploying" >> $LOGFILE
```

This script, written in bash, will be fired after the push is received by the remote repository. It manages the entire deployment process for us by enabling and disabling the maintenance mode and updating the code. Let's look at this more closely:

```
read oldrev newrev refname
```

Here, we store the three arguments passed to the `post-receive` script when it's called. These are as follows:

- The previous commit `SHA1` hash
- The latest commit `SHA1` hash
- The `refname` argument (containing branch information)

This helps us to track what's being deployed, and roll back, if necessary. However, this script doesn't handle a rollback:

```
LOGFILE=./post-receive.log
DEPLOYDIR=/var/www/html/mySite
MAINTENANCE=.htaccess_maintenance
```

Next, we set up a variable to log the output of the deployment and deployment directory:

```
echo -e "Incoming Push at $( date +%F )" >> $LOGFILE
echo " - Old SHA: $oldrev New SHA: $newrev Branch Name: $refname" >> $LOGFILE
```

Here, we log when a push request and its details are received:

```
GIT_WORK_TREE="$DEPLOYDIR" git checkout -f
```

Here, we tell Git where the working tree is, and instruct Git to check out the latest copy of the code in the directory, removing any changes that might have been made manually:

```
echo "Finished Deploying" >> $LOGFILE
```

The last step is to indicate that the deployment is now complete. Of course, this is just an example, and you can do much more:

- Clearing cache folder
- Migrating database
- Running tests
- Changing permissions on folders
- Notifying someone or external services

You can change this hook to suit your needs, and don't forget to make the file executable, otherwise it won't run. If you're not familiar with this process, this is how it's done:

```
Erik@server~:$ chmod +x post-receive
```

Customizing Git

As you already know, when you install Git, you have to configure your username and e-mail, but this isn't the only one configuration you can do:

```
Erik@server~:$ git config --global user.name 'Erik'
Erik@server~:$ git config --global user.email 'erik@mymail.com'
```

Git uses a series of configuration files to perform various activities. First, Git checks the /etc/gitconfig file that contains configurations for every user.

Then, Git looks in ~/.gitconfig, which is specific to each user. Finally, Git checks the .git/config file inside the repository.

There are a lot of options available, but we will cover only the commonly used. You can see a list of all options executing this:

```
Erik@server~:$ git config -help
```

You will find a lot of options to play with, but here are the most important ones:

- **Editor**: You can use editors such as Emacs, Vi, nano, and so on. The following example shows how to use your favorite editor:

    ```
    Erik@server~:$ git config --global core.editor nano
    ```

- **Commit template**: You can specify a message when you commit something:

    ```
    Erik@server~:$ git config --global commit.template ~/gitmsg.txt
    ```

    It will display your template just before the commit information.

- **Autocorrect**: When you type a wrong command, Git will try to understand which command you actually meant to type:

```
Erik@server~:$ git pul
Git : 'pul' is not a git-command. See 'git --help'.
Did you mean this ?
    Pull
```

If you set `help.autorrect` to 1, Git will run the `match` command.

- **Add colors**: You are now forced to use a white font inside your terminal. To add colors, enable it with this command:

```
Erik@server~:$ git config --global color.ui true
```

You can also provide specific colors for each command, but we will not see this here.

Summary

In this chapter, we saw how to work with Git inside an SVN environment, and this it is a great way to enjoy Git's features without migrating all repositories. We saw how to find something inside your Git repository and resolve mistakes. However, when your team is ready to migrate, I encourage you to migrate the most-used repository.

We then saw how to migrate an SVN repository to Git step by step; it's an easy-to-reproduce guide.

The last thing we saw in this chapter was how to use Git submodules, which can be interesting to separate parts of your code.

In the next chapter, we will see how to use Git inside an agile environment along with best practices to build a flexible branching system, and we will use Continuous Integration.

5
Using Git for Continuous Integration

In the previous four chapters, we talked about Git's features, from its most common uses to the most complex ways to use it. However, if this book ends with the previous chapter, it will only be a guide to use Git.

My aim, as an author, is to show you how to use Git to be more efficient in your development. The point of this chapter is to see various approaches to use Git and understand how important Git is to your workflow.

So, in this last chapter, we will see how to:

- Create specific branches to improve your workflow
- Use Git inside an agile environment
- Work with Continuous Integration
- Use other Git tools

Creating an efficient branching system

In the previous chapters, we saw that Git is very useful when you work within a team. Each developer can work locally, and all the work is merged at a remote place.

When you work on a project using a repository, it will be released sooner rather than later. It will be simple if your work stops here, but your project will probably have some bugs that you will have to fix, and you will also have to add some more features.

Your project evolves over time, and working on the **Master** branch will only create serious conflicts. However, don't panic, most Git users already encountered this problem.

The best approach is to leave the **Master** branch as the latest stable version of your repository and develop the branching system around it.

Now, we will see how the Git community tried to avoid using only the **Master** branch.

Git flow

In 2010, a Dutch iOS developer, Vincent Driessen, published the article *Git flow*. In this article, he presents how he sets up his branch model.

His branching strategy starts by creating two main branches:

- Master
- Dev

The **Master** branch is the main branch of the project and will be in the ready-for-production state. They are on the remote repository (origin).

So, whenever you clone the repository on the **Master** branch, you will have the last stable version of the project, which is very important.

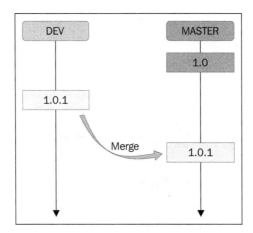

The **dev** branch reflects all the new features for the next release.

When the code inside the **dev** branch is stable (this means that you have done all changes for the next releases and tested it), you reach the stable point on the **dev** branch. Then, you can merge the **dev** branch into **Master**.

Around these two branches, Vincent Driessen also used other branches that can be categorized into three types:

- Feature branches
- Release branches
- Hotfix branches

Feature branches

A feature branch is named based on what your feature is about and will exist as long as the feature is in development.

Feature branches only exist in local developer repositories; do not push them on the remote repository. When your feature is ready, you can merge your branch feature to develop and delete the branch. Execute the following steps:

1. Go back to the **dev** branch:

   ```
   Erik@Server:~/myproject$ git checkout dev
   ```

2. Merge the branch to **dev** by creating a new commit object:

   ```
   Erik@Server:~/myproject$ git merge --no-ff featureBranch
   ```

3. Delete the branch (the branch explains a feature that is now part of the **dev** branch, so there is no reason to keep it):

   ```
   Erik@Server:~/myproject$ git branch -d featureBranch
   ```

4. Push your changes on the remote **dev** repository:

   ```
   Erik@Server:~/myproject$ git push origin dev
   ```

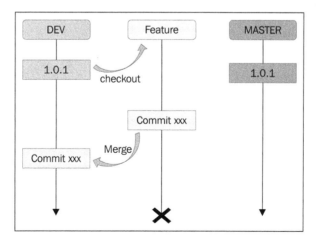

Release branches

You will use the release branch to update your code for minor changes between two big releases. It's named the version number of the project.

At this point, an example will be necessary to explain the process.

Let's imagine that we released our website and it is tagged as Version 1.0. We are working on the next big release that will include a blog. While developing your next great feature on a feature branch called "blog", you have a minor bug on production.

So, we create a release branch from the dev branch, which we will name "release-1.1":

```
Erik@Server:~/myproject$ git checkout -b release-1.1 dev
```

We can fix this bug, but before releasing it, there is a tricky part. Fortunately, this is easy to understand.

First, you have to merge this branch release into master:

```
Erik@Server:~/myproject$ git checkout master
Erik@Server:~/myproject$ git merge --no-ff release-1.1
```

Then, you can tag your project to the new release version:

```
Erik@Server:~/myproject$ git tag -a 1.1
```

You will probably notice that your dev branch didn't include the changes!

To fix this, you have to merge it into the dev:

```
Erik@Server:~/myproject$ git checkout dev
Erik@Server:~/myproject$ git merge --no-ff release-1.1
```

When it's done, delete the release branch:

```
Erik@Server:~/myproject$ git branch -d release-1.1
```

The diagram shows what we have done with the previous commands:

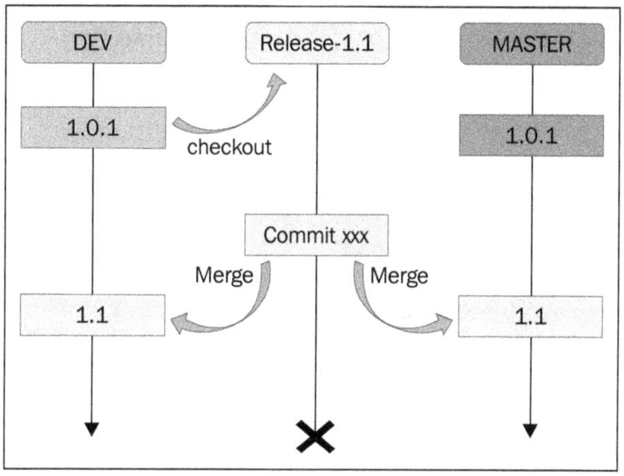

Hotfix branches

These kinds of branches are very similar to release branches. It will respond to fixing a critical bug on production.

The goal is to quickly fix a bug while the other team members can work on their features. For example, your website is tagged as 1.1, and you are still developing the blog feature on the blog branch. You find a huge bug on the slider inside the main page, so you work on the release branch to fix it as soon as possible.

Create a hotfix branch named:

```
Erik@Server:~/myproject$ git checkout -b hotfix-1.1.1 master
```

Fix the bug and merge it to master (after a commit, of course):

```
Erik@Server:~/myproject$ git checkout master
Erik@Server:~/myproject$ git merge --no-ff hotfix-1.1.1
Erik@Server:~/myproject$ git tag -a 1.1.1
```

Similarly, like the release branch, merge the hotfix branch into the current release branch (if it exists) or dev branch. Then delete it:

```
Erik@Server:~/myproject$ git checkout dev
Erik@Server:~/myproject$ git merge --no-ff hotfix-1.1.1
Erik@Server:~/myproject$ git branch -d hotfix-1.1.1
```

The following is an overview of what we have done:

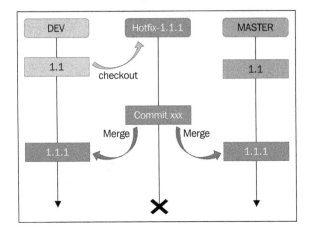

The following table shows the different branches you should create if you choose to implement the Git flow strategy:

Branches	Aim	Naming convention	Created from	Merge into	Delete it after merging?
Master	Production state	master	-	-	No
Dev	Features for the next big release	dev	Master	Master	No
Feature	Creating a new feature	Name of the feature	Dev	Master and Dev	Yes
Release	Minor changes between two big releases	Name of the current project versions 1.1, 1.2, and so on	Dev	Master and Dev	Yes
Hotfix	To fix critical bugs on production	Name of the current versions 1.1.1, 2.1.3, and so on	Master	Master, Release, or Dev	Yes

In summer of 2011, Scott Chacon from GitHub wrote an article about Git flow and spoke about how this branching system didn't fit the development model of GitHub.

The message to take away from his article is that there is no typical branching system for all projects, but you have to find your own approach that fits your project the best.

For example, if you are developing something for a client and there are no new features and only Version 1.0 and hotfixes, using the Git flow model is useless; use only the master for production and dev to commit patches.

BPF – Branch Per Feature

As mentioned earlier, Git flow might suit your project when you use a GitHub project, but the is not always the case.

This model was described by Adam Dymitruk in 2012. He tried to combine the power of Git with Continuous Integration, which is the next topic of this chapter.

In this article, he gave some tips for a more efficient branching strategy:

- Divide your project into several sprints.
- For each sprint, there are several features to develop.
- The features should be small. Develop a small part of the feature, and for each of them, create a dedicated feature branch. So, there will be a lot of branches with few commits in it.
- Merge your branch to the dev branch when it's ready.
- Use a Continuous Integration tool on a Quality Assurance branch so that you will be notified sooner when something is wrong on your feature.
- When it passes the tests, your QA branch is merged into master and you just have to tag the new version.

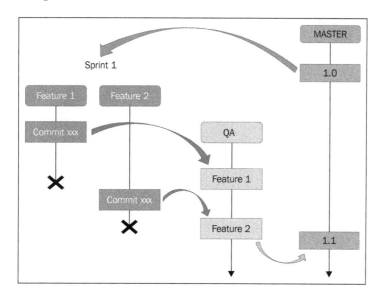

[Every time you start a sprint, create the feature branches and QA.]

The aim of this strategy is:

- All your work is split under feature branches.
- All feature branches start from master (from the last release). When you start a sprint, you create your feature branches at the same time.
- Test your code sooner.

[The QA branch is like the **Dev** branch from Git flow; you shouldn't deploy it, but you have to recreate it on every release.]

Working with Continuous Integration using Git

Working with **Continuous Integration** (CI) means that you need to combine the work frequently and push features as soon as they are ready.

The aim of this way of thinking is that by deploying features when they are ready, your features will be delivered to the customer faster.

There is another good thing: if you deploy on each feature, the deployment will be smaller, so it will generate less problems because you have less things to test on each release.

This model is the practical way of using Scrum. You start a project, separate it into several sprints, divide the sprints into small features, and you are ready to start. This is the age-old policy of divide and rule.

As we already saw in the previous chapters, Git is powerful and excels at branching and merging. So, you can easily implement an agile model using Git.

To fulfill these principles, you have to integrate the changes locally. Then, you have to be sure that this code will work everywhere by pushing it into a private branch on the integration machine. If the test fails, go back to your local machine, fix the bugs, and test it again on the integration machine.

When successful, you can promote your code to a public branch. However, if someone integrates the code while you are testing yours, you will have to start testing again.

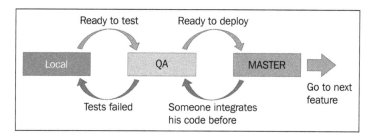

I encourage you to read more about these strategies if you are interested, because I choose to resume the known ones. There are, of course, other strategies, some of which are more complicated but are very interesting. Examples include Squash workflow, Oxygen workflow, and so on. Every big company has its own branching systems, which are variants of Git flow.

Git tools you might like

To end this chapter, I choose to present to you some tools around Git that you can probably use, or might prompt you to research further.

It can be rewarding to finish this book with an opening to other related topics, which will push you to always learn more.

Git GUI clients

A nice way to start this presentation for cons-terminal is to use the GUI clients for all operating systems. I am aware that there are a lot of clients for each OS, but I will show the most-used clients.

On Linux

Lot of Linux users like to use Git through command lines or their code editors, but there are GUI tools too for all developers:

- **Git-cola**: This software is developed in Python and has the usual pull, push, and commit functions. It also has a diff viewer. The following screenshot shows the interface of Git-cola:

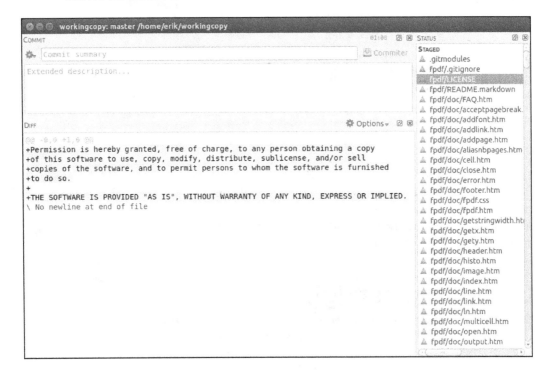

- **Gitg**: This tool is very simple and colorful; you will get a graphical display of your repository. You will also get a diff viewer and file browser. The following screenshot shows the interface of Gitg:

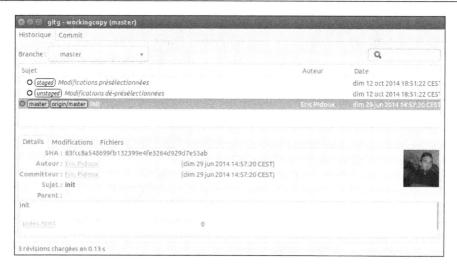

On Windows

The following are the GUI tools for Windows:

- **TortoiseGit**: This is similar to TortoiseSvn for those who use SVN on Windows. Its most popular feature is that it's integrated into the Windows Context menu, so you can perform Git commands inside the Windows explorer.

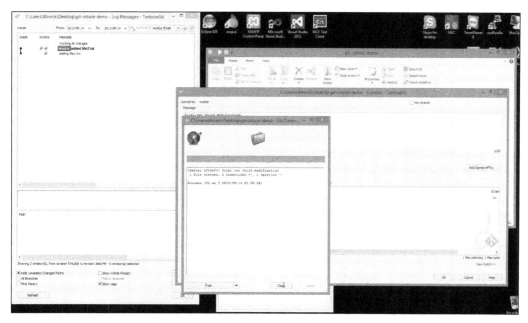

The interface of TortoiseGit

- **GitHub Client**: GitHub released a tool that you can easily use with your GitHub repository or even something else. This tool can be very interesting if you are using GitHub exclusively as a repository manager because it is nicer and easy to use. The following screenshot shows the interface of GitHub Client:

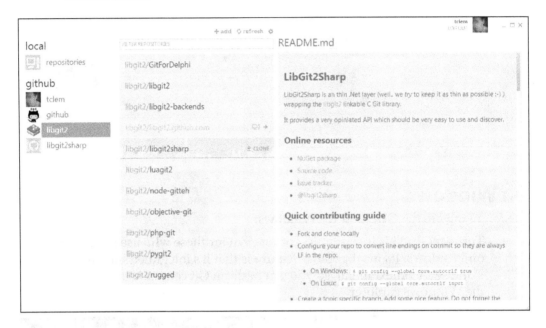

- **msysGit**: This tool is a little bit uglier, but as practical as others, and you can use the Windows CMD shell too. It comes with its own SSH. The following screenshot shows the interface of msysGit:

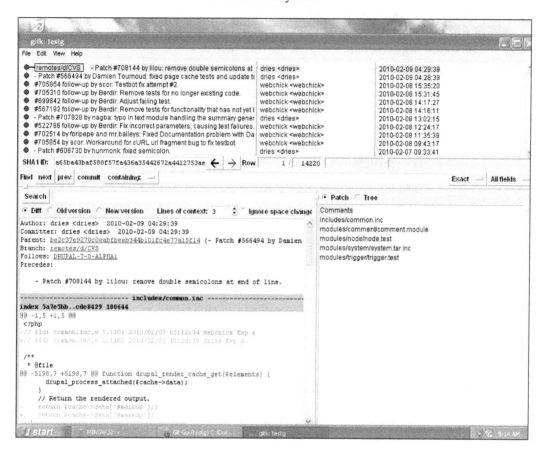

On Mac

The following are the GUI tools for Mac:

- **GitX**: This is the most popular open-source tool for Mac. There are a lot of forks of this tool, such as GitX – Pieter, GitX(L), and GitX – Rowanj. The following screenshot shows the interface of GitX:

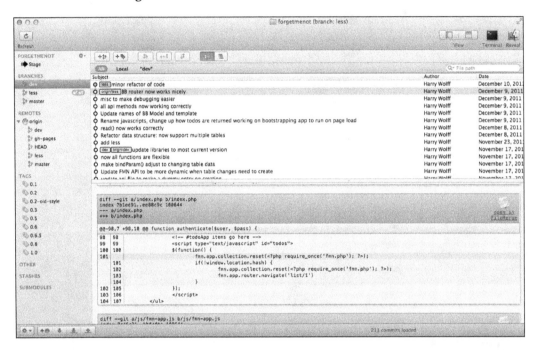

- **Gitbox**: This tool is also a fork of GitX, but it's faster and more intuitive than the original and includes all the necessary features. The following screenshot shows the interface of Gitbox:

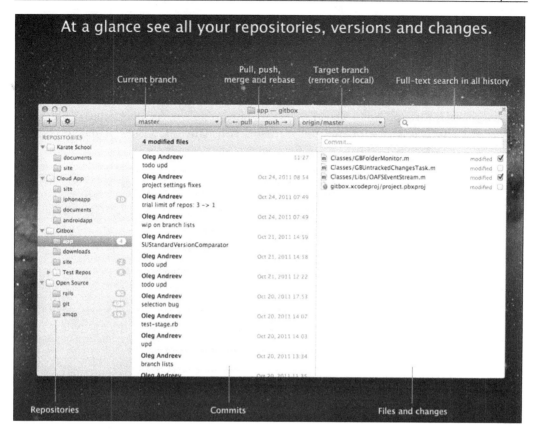

Mac has a GitHub client, too. However, you can also use a Git plugin directly inside your IDE (Eclipse, NetBeans, PhpStorm, Sublime Text, and so on).

Repository management

A repository manager is a tool that helps you to manage your Git repository. It's often a remote web-based tool on which you can manage user rights on all your repositories, explore the files and the commit history, manage branches, tags, and so on.

I will introduce you two famous Git repositories. The first one is well-known and used by a lot of developers and the last one second is open source and could be self-hosted:

- **GitHub**: GitHub is a Git repository web-based hosting application. It offers revision control and code management. It has free accounts for public repositories and paid plans for private ones. You can connect external services such as Travis CI for Continuous Integration. The following screenshot shows the interface of GitHub:

- **GitLab**: GitLab is the same as GitHub. The great thing about this tool is that you install it on your own server and have unlimited repositories, users, and so on.

  GitLab has purpose-free and paid plans on its website if you don't want to have them on your server. The following screenshot shows the interface of GitLab:

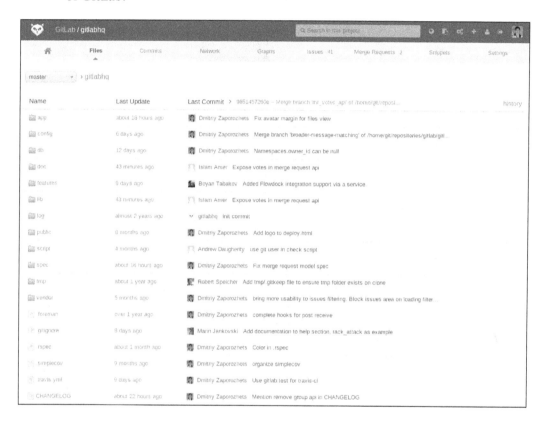

Summary

In this chapter, we saw a nice way of using Git inside an agile environment. It might not be useful for you, but I hope this information will prompt you to ask yourself about how you can use Git to be more efficient and responsive.

The last part of this chapter is a bit sharp, but there are thousands of Git GUI clients or Git repository management applications available, and you should find the one that best suits your purposes.

If you don't find one, there will always be the timeless and matchless terminal!

Index

F

fast forward merge 20, 21
feature branches 67
file, Git repository
  adding 8
  committing 8, 9
  ignoring 12
  pushing 9, 10
  removing 10
  status, checking 10, 11
Fixup option, rebase command 25

G

Git
  configuring 5
  customizing 62
  existent repository, cloning 6
  repository, initializing 5, 6
  used, for working with Continuous
      Integration (CI) 72, 73
git bisect command 40, 41
Gitbox 78
git clean command 36
Git-cola 74
git diff command 33
git filter-branch 38
git format-patch command
  about 55
  using 56
Gitg 74
Git GUI clients
  about 73
  on Linux 74
  on Mac 78
  on Windows 75
Git hooks
  about 57, 58
  client hooks 57
  commit-msg 58
  example 60, 61
  installing 59
  post-checkout 58
  post-commit 58
  post-merge 58

post-receive 58
post-update 58
pre-commit 58
pre-receive 58
server hooks 57, 58
update 58
GitHub
  about 48, 80
  URL 48
GitHub Client 76
GitLab 81
git log command
  about 31
  executing 46
git merge command 20
Git repository
  file, adding 8
  file, committing 8, 9
  file, pushing 9, 10
  file, removing 10
  files, ignoring 12
  GitHub 80
  GitLab 81
  MODIFIED state 7
  STAGED state 7
  status, checking 10, 11
  UNMODIFIED state 7
  UNTRACKED state 7
  working with 7
git reset command
  --hard option 36
  --mixed option 36
  --soft option 36
  about 35
git revert command 38
git show command 34
git stash command 34
git status command 30
Git submodules
  adding 51
  managing 51
  removing 53
  used, for cloning project 52
Git subtree 54
Git SVN
  working with 50

R

rebase command
  --interactive option 25
  about 23, 25
  Edit option 25
  Exec option 25
  Fixup option 25
  Pick option 25
  Reword option 25
  Squash option 25
recursive strategy, merging strategies 23
Refs directory file 6
release branches 68, 69
remote repositories
  data, pushing on 16
repository management 79
repository manager 79
Reword option, rebase command 25

S

Secure Shell (SSH) protocol
  about 14, 15
  cons 15
  pros 15
server hooks 58
server repository
  creating 13, 14
  Git transport 15
  HTTPS protocol 16
  local protocol 14
  Secure Shell (SSH) protocol 14

Squash option, rebase command 25
stat option 55
stat parameter 32
subtree
  contributing on 54
  subproject, adding with 54
  using 53
SVN to Git migration
  about 45
  branches, migrating 47, 48
  commits, cleaning 47
  content, pushing on Git 47
  performing 45, 46
  preparing for 46
  tags, migrating 47, 48

T

tags
  creating 26
  deleting 26
  using 26
theirs strategy, merging strategies 23
TortoiseGit 75

U

update hook
  variables 59

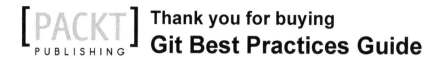

Thank you for buying
Git Best Practices Guide

About Packt Publishing

Packt, pronounced 'packed', published its first book "*Mastering phpMyAdmin for Effective MySQL Management*" in April 2004 and subsequently continued to specialize in publishing highly focused books on specific technologies and solutions.

Our books and publications share the experiences of your fellow IT professionals in adapting and customizing today's systems, applications, and frameworks. Our solution based books give you the knowledge and power to customize the software and technologies you're using to get the job done. Packt books are more specific and less general than the IT books you have seen in the past. Our unique business model allows us to bring you more focused information, giving you more of what you need to know, and less of what you don't.

Packt is a modern, yet unique publishing company, which focuses on producing quality, cutting-edge books for communities of developers, administrators, and newbies alike. For more information, please visit our website: www.packtpub.com.

Writing for Packt

We welcome all inquiries from people who are interested in authoring. Book proposals should be sent to author@packtpub.com. If your book idea is still at an early stage and you would like to discuss it first before writing a formal book proposal, contact us; one of our commissioning editors will get in touch with you.

We're not just looking for published authors; if you have strong technical skills but no writing experience, our experienced editors can help you develop a writing career, or simply get some additional reward for your expertise.

Git Version Control Cookbook

ISBN: 978-1-78216-845-4   Paperback: 340 pages

90 hands-on recipes that will increase your productivity when using Git as a version control system

1. Filled with practical recipes that will teach you how to use the most advanced features of the Git system.

2. Improve your productivity by learning to work faster, more efficiently, and with more confidence.

3. Discover tips and tricks that will show you when and how to use the advanced features of Git.

Git: Version Control for Everyone Beginner's Guide

ISBN: 978-1-84951-752-2   Paperback: 180 pages

The non-coder's guide to everyday version control for increased efficiency and productivity

1. A complete beginner's workflow for version control of common documents and content.

2. Examples used are from nontechie, day-to-day computing activities we all engage in.

3. Learn through multiple modes—readers learn theories to understand the concept and reinforce it by practical tutorials.

GitLab Repository Management

ISBN: 978-1-78328-179-4   Paperback: 88 pages

Delve into managing your projects with GitLab, while tailoring it to fit your environment

1. Understand how to efficiently track and manage projects.

2. Establish teams with a fast software developing tool.

3. Employ teams constructively in a GitLab environment.

Mastering Object-oriented Python

ISBN: 978-1-78328-097-1   Paperback: 634 pages

Grasp the intricacies of object-oriented programming in Python in order to efficiently build powerful real-world applications

1. Create applications with flexible logging, powerful configuration and command-line options, automated unit tests, and good documentation.

2. Use Python's special methods to integrate seamlessly with built-in features and the standard library.

3. Design classes to support object persistence in JSON, YAML, Pickle, CSV, XML, Shelve, and SQL.

Please check **www.PacktPub.com** for information on our titles